3 ARTIFICIAL INTELLIGENCE

ARTIFICIAL INTELLIGENCE

A.M. ANDREW

Viable Systems
Chillaton, Devon (U.K.)

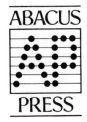

ABACUS
PRESS

First published in 1983 by

ABACUS PRESS

Abacus House, Speldhurst Road, Tunbridge Wells, Kent TN4 0HU

British Library Cataloguing in Publication Date
Andrew, A.M.
    Artificial intelligence.
    1. Artificial intelligence
    I. Title
    001.53′5 Q335

    ISBN 0-85626-165-3

Typesetting by Permanent Typesetting & Printing Co., Ltd., Hong Kong
and printed and bound in Malta by Interprint Ltd

CYBERNETICS AND SYSTEMS SERIES

Editor in Chief

J. ROSE

Director-General,
World Organisation of General Systems and Cybernetics

Already Published

1. Philosophical Foundations of Cybernetics
2. Fuzzy Systems
5. Economic Cybernetics
6. Cybernetics and Society
11. Computers and Cybernetics

Other Titles in Preparation

4. Management Cybernetics
7. Models and Modelling of Systems
8. Automation and Cybernetics
9. Medical Cybernetics
10. General System Theory
12. Neurocybernetics
13. Metamodels and Metasystems

SERIES PREFACE

The inter- and trans-disciplinary sciences of cybernetics and systems have made tremendous advances in the last two decades. Hundreds of books have been published dealing with various aspects of these sciences. In addition, a variety of specialist journals and voluminous post-conference reports have appeared, and learned societies, national and international, established. These substantial advances reflect the course of the Second Industrial Revolution, otherwise known as the Cybernetics Revolution.

In order to acquaint readers with advances in these sciences which are rapidly achieving tremendous importance and which impinge upon many aspects of our life and society, it was considered essential to produce a series of concise and readable monographs, each concerned with one particular aspect. The twelve topics constituting the first series are as follows (in alphabetical order).

Artificial Intelligence, Automation and Cybernetics, Computers and Cybernetics, Cybernetics and Society, Economic Cybernetics, Fuzzy Systems, General System Theory, Management Cybernetics, Medical Cybernetics, Models and Modelling of Systems, Neurocybernetics, Philosophical Foundations of Cybernetics.

The authors are experts in their particular fields and of great repute. The emphasis is on intelligible presentation without excess mathematics and abstract matter. It is hoped each monograph will become standard reading matter at academic institutions and among informed scientists. In this age of enormous scientific advances and of uncertainty concerning the welfare of societies and the very future of mankind, it is vital to obtain a sound insight into the issues involved, to help us to understand the present and face the future with greater confidence.

J. ROSE
Blackburn

PREFACE

In this book I have tried to describe the main achievements under the heading of Artificial Intelligence, with comments on their relationship to other fields of study. These include Computer Science, in which many important developments have been stimulated by the needs of Artificial Intelligence. They also include Psychology and Neurophysiology, the latter being most closely associated with the "Cybernetic" or "self-organizing system" approach to Artificial Intelligence. The relationship of this to the "mainstream" studies is discussed.

I have indulged freely in long-term speculation about future developments, and discussion of ultimate limitations. I have also referred to the relatively short-term significance of current work, and this is an aspect which can well be given further emphasis. Now that microprocessors are with us, computers are coming more and more into everyday life, either in their own right in homes and businesses or incorporated in cars, washing machines and like. Cheap and portable systems of sufficient power to allow implementation of A.I. techniques are certainly on the way. These will have eyes and ears and will control robot arms. Not only will computers be familiar in everyday life, they will participate in it in an increasingly human-like way. Already there are mini-computers which play a powerful game of chess, and talk of Expert Systems to be carried in the pocket.

Much of the material I had previously assembled in order to give lectures in Reading University. I have taken advantage of my wife's position in the Psychology Department there to make considerable use of the facilities of that Department, and particularly to seek advice from Mrs. Yvonne Robinson on the preparation of illustrations. My wife Joyce has helped me in very many ways — working on the figures, making valuable suggestions about content and presentation, and checking my spelling — all while busy with other work of her own. Whatever the quality of my effort, it is certainly much improved by her participation.

A.M. ANDREW
Viable Systems (U.K.)

CONTENTS

Chapter 1

WHAT IS ARTIFICIAL INTELLIGENCE?

What is studied under the heading of *Artificial Intelligence* is ways of making machines behave intelligently. To delimit the subject area more precisely it is necessary to consider what is meant by *intelligence* and hence what constitutes intelligent behaviour. It is also necessary to say something about what may be meant by a *machine* in the modern context, though this is a much more straightforward matter than the attempt to define intelligence. There is, in fact, no satisfactory objective definition of the latter, and although the matter will be discussed here it will finally be necessary to fall back on intuition, aided by a listing of some areas of investigation that have customarily been subsumed under Artificial Intelligence.

Usually, in this context, the word *machine* denotes a program running on a general-purpose digital computer. Sometimes special-purpose electronic devices have been built, but these are essentially computer-like. Such "machines" have a very different character from that of the relatively brute-force machines of the Industrial Revolution. There is, however, a tendency in recent years for the machines of Artificial Intelligence to become increasingly "muscular." The subdivision of A.I. termed *Robotics* considers the use of intelligent machines to manipulate objects in the real world.

WHAT IS INTELLIGENCE?

Psychologists are usually wary of committing themselves to definitions of *intelligence*. One has remarked that the only consistent definition is as "whatever it is that intelligence tests measure". Some workers in A.I. have followed the lead of this definition and have written programs which solve problems of types used in intelligence tests.

A definition couched in more general terms is clearly to be preferred, and intelligence has sometimes been defined as the capacity to respond appropriately in a novel situation. Some experiments designed to test the intelligence of animals are very much in accordance with this definition. For example, a monkey may be placed in a room in which a banana is hung at a height too great for the monkey to reach. In the room there is a box which, if placed under the banana, gives the monkey the necessary extra height. If the monkey drags the box so that it is under the banana, and then stands on it to secure the fruit, it is showing intelligence. Other more complicated situations have been devised, requiring the monkey to "fish" for the fruit using a stick, or to join two sticks together to fish at a greater distance.

The kind of "intelligence" revealed by these tests is close to our intuitive understanding of the term, but the definition is not completely objective. Subjective judgement is needed to decide whether a situation is "novel" in the right sort of way. A pocket calculator set to multiply two numbers is probably faced with a situation that is, for it, novel; if the numbers are large and are not well-known ones like *pi* or the number of inches in a mile, the chances are that the calculator has never before been set to multiply them. Nevertheless, it is not usually held to be "intelligent" because it responds appropriately in this novel situation. The situation does not have the same qualitative novelty as does the monkey-box-banana one, but it is difficult to express this distinction in objective terms.

The attempt to define "intelligence" is equivalent to the attempt to define "thinking" in trying to answer the question "Can machines think?". The whole subject of A.I. can be said to be the attempt to answer this question. The fact that most people, nowadays, would not describe a pocket calculator as "intelligent" or "thinking" illustrates the important point that any attempt to make an intelligent or thinking machine is automatically self-defeating. The very fact that some behaviour *is* exhibited by a machine causes people to say "That isn't what we mean by thinking — we see how a machine can do it." Until Artificial Intelligence achieves the ultimate goal of duplicating every aspect of human intelligence (a goal that is beyond the reasonably foreseeable future) it must have this self-defeating character. Like a person chasing the end of the rainbow it can never reach its goal, though it may discover other treasures on the way. Our forebears of a few generations back would readily have ascribed "intelligence" (probably demonaical) to a pocket calculator, but now a machine has to do much more to qualify.

Artificial Intelligence, then, is an area of study in which there is the attempt to make machines do things it is currently difficult to make them do, especially things that can be seen to be done by people. The inclusion of "currently difficult" shows this to be a shifting definition, just as the idea of what constitutes a "thinking machine" shifts as the state-of-the-art advances. Because it has embarked on this never-ending quest, and because many capable people have been attracted to work in it, Artificial Intelligence has been a spearhead of developments in Computer Science. This is discussed at greater length in Chapter 13.

An interesting attempt to say what might be meant by a "thinking machine" was made by the mathematician and computer scientist Alan Turing[1]. This is referred to as the "Interrogation Game" (*see* F.H.George, *Philosophical Foundations of Cybernetics*, vol. 1 of this series). Turing must have attended some very tedious parties, for he introduces his ideas by referring to a party game which requires some member of the company to retire secretly to another room. The other guests are then invited to interrogate the absentee and to try to decide from the replies whether they are communicating with a man or a woman. It is, of course, necessary that the replies are not spoken directly. They must either be written down or conveyed by an intermediary. (Alternatively, a teleprinter link could be used, if available.)

Turing's idea was to test a machine, purported to be intelligent, by letting it be similarly interrogated. If the interrogator is unable to decide whether he has been interacting with a person or a machine, and in fact it was the machine, the machine should be accepted as "intelligent".

Existing computer programs may be said to have passed Turing's test in simple ways. Some game-playing programs (Chapters 5 and 6) are sufficiently human-like in their responses that some of their human opponents have been sure they were playing against a hidden person. There is a well-known computer program called *ELIZA* which plays the part of a psychiatrist (Chapter 9). Patients who were "interviewed" by this program were often quite sure they had been in communication with a real doctor.

These programs, however, were not simulating an entire human being prepared to converse on various subjects, which is presumably what Turing had in mind. Game-playing programs obviously correspond to humans behaving in a very restricted fashion. The *ELIZA* program can simulate a psychiatrist determined (as some real psychiatrists are) to avoid "priming" his patient by supplying any morsel of information to him.

Computer programs can effectively simulate human beings behaving in a restricted fashion. The fact that real human beings sometimes choose to impose restrictions on themselves makes Turing's test somewhat ambiguous. The test may also be felt to be unsatisfactory in that it emphasises the *simulation* of intelligence rather than the achievement of any useful or potentially-useful result (however, see the closing remarks of Chapter 15).

IS ARTIFICIAL INTELLIGENCE POSSIBLE?

The reader may now be persuaded that *Artificial Intelligence* denotes an important area of study — it must be, if it is truly a spearhead of developments in Computer Science — but there are two fundamental questions that have not been answered. These are as follows:

(a) Do the techniques subsumed under *Artificial Intelligence* truly imitate a significant part of what we intuitively understand by *intelligence*? In other words, is the term *Artificial Intelligence* warranted?

(b) Are there aspects of human intelligence that cannot *ever* be imitated by machines?

Of course, question (a) is very like the one raised earlier — "Can machines think?" Like that question, it is highly imprecise, depending on the intuitive idea of "intelligence" as well as other imprecise terms. Since the question is imprecise, it is necessary when considering it to guard against the previously-mentioned tendency to disallow a form of operation as a manifestation of intelligence simply because it has been exhibited by a machine.

In specific task-environments, such as chess-playing, it is possible to compare human and machine performance. It has been cogently argued, notably by H.L. Dreyfus, that there are whole areas of human performance that machine performance comes nowhere near to imitating. For the present discussion it is, of course, best to postpone any attempt at comparison until some of the achievements of Artificial Intelligence studies have been described (see Chapters 13 and 14).

There is, however, an aspect of the matter that can usefully be discussed at this point, namely the question whether machines can achieve *innovation*. Although it is possible to trace the origins of Artificial Intelligence earlier than the advent of electronic digital computers (for example, in chess-playing and other automata), modern work in A.I. is almost totally based on digital computing. This is hardly surprising since digital computers, are, in some important ways, much more brain-like than any other artefacts. They are the most complex devices ever produced artificially. They also share with the brain a degree of generality that makes it very difficult to make any precise statement about the capabilities of either.

On the other hand, there is a way of looking at computers that suggests they are bound to be morons. All they can do is follow the steps of a program prepared for them by a human programmer. Certainly, the programmer has the possibility of arranging "choice points" in the program, such that the subsequent sequence of operations is chosen from two or more alternatives, the choice depending on the results of previous computations. The general idea is, nevertheless, the same; the computer blindly follows a sequence of operations prearranged by the human programmer. It seems impossible that such a moronic device could ever be credited with any kind of "intelligence". The latter is generally held to imply "innovation" (also a difficult idea to pin down in precise terms). To suggest that a programmed device may be innovative seems to be a contradiction in terms.

Computers have always been seen in two disparate ways, as whimsically indicated by Hofstadter's[2] term for them of "smartstupids". When the first digital computers were built, the popular press referred to them by such terms as "giant brains". Responsible scientists felt obliged to present a more sober view, emphasising the moronic nature of the machines. Many of these scientists modified their viewpoint some years later when computers and programming techniques had been further developed.

There is no getting away from the fact that a computer *is* a moronic program-follower, but when the computer and program become sufficiently complex the behaviour may be unpredictable in practice though predictable in principle. It is not, therefore, nonsense to regard the machine as potentially innovative. If there is no simpler way of predicting the behaviour of a machine than actually running it (or another of similar complexity) to see what happens, the limitation to predictable behaviour becomes somewhat irrelevant. In fact, the human brain may be "predictable" (except for random-noise effects — see later); it is possible that, if we knew the characteristics of every neuron (nerve cell) in a brain, their pattern of interconnections, and for some instant in time, their states of excitation, the future behaviour of the brain could be predicted. It is therefore, to say the least, far from clear that the predictable nature of digital machinery necessarily debars it from exhibiting intelligence and innovation.

The word "predictable" has been used somewhat loosely in the above; it has been implicitly assumed that the input signals to the machine or brain could be predicted, possibly on the basis of earlier outputs. There are formal ways of representing systems that are predictable in the required sense. If they have a finite amount of storage they can be represented as *finite automata*; where the amount is unlimited they must be equivalent to a *Turing machine*. A computer program is a finite automaton, almost by definition. (See Appendix 1 to this chapter, also Chapter 10 of F.H. George's book in this series. Professor George discusses these philosophical aspects of machine and artificial intelligence in greater detail than will be attempted here).

Finite automata and Turing machines are necessarily deterministic systems; they are not affected by unpredictable effects such as random noise. There is evidence that the brain *is* affected by random disturbances. The threshold for excitation of a neuron undergoes seemingly-random fluctuations, and it is believed that neurons in the brain, presumably at random, simply die and are not replaced. (Delisle Burns has estimated that, in an adult human brain, one hundred thousand nerve cells die every day.) Artificial systems can also be affected by random noise, so it cannot be claimed that this, in itself, distinguishes brains from machines. It does, however, distinguish brains from programs on most digital computers since the latter are carefully designed to be deterministic, that is to say, unaffected by random effects.

Some early computers escaped the restriction to deterministic operation by embodying sources of truly-random numbers, generated from some unpredictable effect such as resistor noise or radioactive disintegration. The operation was deterministic except when a program incorporated an instruction of a particular type to introduce a random number.

Modern digital computers do not embody sources of truly-random numbers. For computational tasks requiring the production of sequences of random-looking numbers it is customary to generate them by computational procedures, the numbers being termed "pseudo-random". They are not truly random since a procedure will always produce numbers from the same cyclic sequence. The procedure is, in fact, an extremely compact way of storing a very long (cyclic) table of random numbers. Since the cycle is very long, the sequence of numbers used in one run of a program is a small fraction of the total, and different sequences are obtained by starting at different points in the cycle. Sometimes it is arranged that the starting-point depends on the indication on the "real-time clock", i.e. the time of day and perhaps the date, at the moment when the first number in the sequence is required in the running of the program. This is a convenient way of arranging that a different sequence is produced every time the program is run, exactly as would happen if the numbers came from a truly-random source.

A note on ways of producing pseudo-random numbers has been included as Appendix 2 to this chapter, so that the nature of this bridge between determinacy and indeterminacy may be seen. Actually, randomness (or pseudo-randomness) is not an important feature of most programs in what may be termed "mainstream" Artificial Intelligence research, but would find greater use in ones escaping from the limitations discussed in Chapter 14, i.e. programs able to develop their own heuristics.

Random or pseudo-random number generation is frequently invoked in programs embodying the "Cybernetic" approach to A.I. It is needed, for example, in implementing both the "conjugation" and the "mutated fission" postulated by Selfridge for his *Pandemonium* (Chapter 7) and in connection with *perceptrons*, especially the variation due to Roberts (Chapter 8). It is also employed in all the methods for producing "Computer Art" discussed in Chapter 11 and is a well-established weapon in the armoury of programmers.

The distinction made in the last paragraph acknowledges that there is a diversity of approaches to A.I., and it is necessary to discuss the relationship of the approaches, and their relationship to Cybernetics.

CYBERNETICS AND ARTIFICIAL INTELLIGENCE

Professor George, in his volume in this series, and elsewhere, has virtually equated Cybernetics with the search for Artificial Intelligence. This viewpoint is in agreement with the definition of Cybernetics appearing as the subtitle of Wiener's book[3], namely "control and communication in the animal and the machine". There can be no doubt that the reference to "the animal" is essential; the main result to be expected from the new science was greater understanding of processes occurring in living organisms and communities of organisms.

Of these processes the working of the brain is that which presents the greatest challenge (not that there is any dearth of unsolved problems at lower levels!).

In considering the meaning, and therefore the origins, of Cybernetics it is appropriate to look to that other great pioneer of the subject, Warren McCulloch. Although Wiener gave the subject its name and formal status by writing his book, many people who were active in the area at the time regard McCulloch as being at least equally deserving of the title "Father of Cybernetics". (These two great thinkers were friends at the time of the formal birth of Cybernetics and it is impossible to distinguish their respective contributions with any precision. The origins of the unfortunate rift that came between them a few years later are now, and were even then, highly obscure.)

McCulloch[4] has attributed the development of Cybernetics to his own attempts to answer the question he posed as "What is a number, that a man may know it, and a man, that he may know a number?". The implications of this question clearly enter the realms of Artificial Intelligence and invoke considerations of epistemology, or the internal representation of the outside world within a nervous system or a machine. McCulloch insisted that the epistemology should be "experimental epistemology"; he sought explanations in terms of the experimentally-demonstrable properties of the nervous system, down to the single-cell level.

Having now seen that Professor George's equation of Cybernetics with the pursuit of Artificial Intelligence is essentially valid, it is rather puzzling to find that many workers in the two areas do not see them as equivalent. Certainly, most workers in the "mainstream" areas of Artificial Intelligence would deny that they are involved in Cybernetics; workers in Cybernetics take a generous view of the coverage of their subject and would view A.I. as a subdivision of it. That the two subject areas are not seen as equivalent is apparent from the choice of topics for the books in the present series; if A.I. and Cybernetics were virtually synonymous it would hardly be appropriate to have one volume specifically devoted to A.I.

As mentioned earlier, there is a diversity of approaches to A.I., perhaps most usefully referred to as a dichotomy since the approaches fall under two main headings. What is now usually understood by A.I. (and has been referred to here as "mainstream" A.I.), is work carried out with no attempt at all to simulate the phenomena of nervous-system activity. Most of the computer programs produced (this work is exclusively carried out using digital computers) embody no facility for learning from experience. They can only be said to simulate human mentation, if at all, at a high level. This, of course, is not to deny their potential value in helping to explicate brain mechanisms; a system of the complexity of the brain has to be examined from many different points of view including, and perhaps primarily, high-level ones.

In the early days of Cybernetics, up to about 1958, the dichotomy of approaches was not evident. Workers in Artificial Intelligence, in the modern "mainstream" sense of the word, regard their subject as taking off from work reported around this time (and thus begun somewhat earlier). Two workers who set the scene for what was to come were Marvin Minsky[5] and John McCarthy[6], the latter the originator of the programming language LISP — see Chapter 13. Minsky was associated with the Massachusetts Institute of Technology, where he was influenced by McCulloch and so is able to straddle the dichotomy of approaches. Other important work in progress at that time included the development of the General Problem Solver by Newell, Shaw and Simon (Chapter 3) and work by Samuel (Chapter 6) and Selfridge (Chapter 7), among others.

The dichotomy of approaches is recognised in the title of an introductory text-book by Slagle[7], entitled *Artificial Intelligence — the Heuristic Programming Approach*. He is, in fact, concerned with what is referred to here as the "mainstream" approach and refers to it in this way for want of a better concise term. The term is appropriate in that *heuristics* are a pervasive ingredient of work adopting the approach.

The dichotomy is also recognised and discussed in the preface of the well-known book by Feigenbaum and Feldman[8]. This is intended as a collection of the most significant papers in the A.I. field at the time of its publication (1963). These authors refer to the "mainstream" or "heuristic programming" approach by the not-very-descriptive term "cognitive models" and contrast it with the "neural cybernetics" or "self-organizing systems" approach. Their comments are as follows:

"Neural cybernetics approaches the problem of designing intelligent machines by postulating a large number of very simple information processing elements, arranged in a random or organized network, and certain processes for facilitating or inhibiting their activity. Cognitive model builders take a much more macroscopic approach, using highly complex information processing mechanisms as the basis of their designs. They believe that intelligent performance by a machine is an end difficult enough to achieve without 'starting from scratch', and so they build into their systems as much complexity of information processing as they are able to understand and communicate to a computer (using their programming techniques)."

Feigenbaum and Feldman go on to compare what has been achieved following each of the approaches and conclude that there is vastly more progress to report on "cognitive models". They claim, in fact, that progress in "neural cybernetics" is (in 1963) "barely discernable". In their reference to networks of simple information-processing elements they are talking about the many attempts to produce "self-organizing systems" intended to learn intelligent behaviour by a learning process while interacting with an environment. The intention of these studies is to model the self-organizing capability of the nervous system, and usually the constituent elements are designed to have some correspondence to the known properties of nerve cells.

Needless to say, the debate between the protagonists of the two approaches continues today. Most of this book will be given over to descriptions of work coming under "heuristic programming" or "cognitive models", if only because, as in 1963, there is much more solid progress to report in this area. It will, however, be argued that there is a need for another approach; the "heuristic programming" one is open to objection on the grounds of its *ad hoc* nature, introducing different techniques in the context of different tasks. Discussion of these general aspects is, of course, best postponed until later chapters, after the description of what has actually been done.

In the meantime it is worth giving attention, perhaps belatedly, to what are the aims of work in Artificial Intelligence.

THE AIMS OF ARTIFICIAL INTELLIGENCE

The attempt to make machines behave as intelligently as possible (whatever is meant by this) has an intrinsic fascination, and it is likely that many workers in the area have not tried to be explicit about their motivation. As for many other research areas, motivations come under the two headings of *explanation* and *exploitation*.

Some A.I. work has been undertaken with the avowed aim of elucidating human thought processes by simulating them in computer programs. Some enthusiasts have even implied that no psychologist worth his salt would try to operate without constructing such models. The work of Newell, Shaw and Simon on their General Problem Solver was intended to model the behaviour of experimental subjects attempting to solve problems. The subjects were asked to talk into a tape-recorder while attempting the tasks, and to record as much of their thinking as they could. The G.P.S. program was then developed as an attempt to model the contents of these recorded "protocols". Of course, the accuracy of the simulation depends on the extent to which the problem-solving process is accessible to introspection and the extent to which it can be described verbally, but more of that anon.

Even where the construction of the program is not an explicit attempt to model experimentally-observed human behaviour, the fact that "intelligence" is meant to be achieved implies a simulation of human performance at some level and hence the possibility of greater understanding of natural intelligence.

Some A.I. programs embody principles that pretty certainly do *not* correspond to the methods used by a person to achieve a similar result. It is generally agreed, for example, that the existing successful programs for playing chess do not simulate the methods of analysis used by human players (Chapter 5). Even here, however, the exploration of problem-solving methods necessary to develop the program may, indirectly, improve understanding of the human method. It is likely to give a feeling for the nature of the problem which makes it possible to rule out some hypotheses about methods that *could* be used by human players. (Extreme caution is needed in applying this kind of argument however; any assessment of the magnitude and nature of the problem must be in relation to the techniques available, and natural evolution has undoubtedly produced tricks that have not occurred to the programmers.)

The other type of motivation is that which can be subsumed under "exploitation". The more "intelligent" machines are, the more useful they become to their owners (assuming, that is, they remain amenable). In recent years (at the time of writing in 1981) the economic recession has led to cut-backs in research funding and A.I. researchers have perforce had to concentrate on projects that could be justified on short-term economic grounds. During this period there has been particular attention to *Robotics*, which has great economic potential, and to Expert Systems, which have applications in medical diagnosis and elsewhere. Various forms of *Pattern Recognition* also have immediate practical value.

TOPICS IN ARTIFICIAL INTELLIGENCE

Reference has been made to various topics, in this chapter and in the Table of Contents. The main areas of A.I. effort are as follows:

Theorem-Proving. This overlaps other areas of automated methematics, and problem-solving in other areas (e.g. *Robotics*).

Game Playing. Chess has received particular attention.

Pattern Recognition. This can refer to visual or auditory patterns, or patterns in other (or mixed) modalities. Medical diagnosis and weather forecasting are tasks of pattern recognition not associated with a particular modality. In much recent work the emphasis is on *scene analysis* rather than the recognition of isolated objects (e.g. printed characters); this is important for *Robotics*.

Use of Natural Language. Question-answering systems and *Mechanical Translation* have received much attention. Recent work by Winograd relates natural language to *Robotics*.

Robotics. This has direct practical importance.

Expert Systems. These embody a great deal of the knowledge and skills of a human expert, and have proved their value in medical diagnosis and elsewhere.

Knowledge Engineering. This is not an area in its own right, but the term reflects a particular way of looking at how different kinds of knowledge must interact in pattern recognition, robotics and expert systems.

Appendix 1.1

FINITE AUTOMATA

An automation may be *finite* in the sense that it can exist in any of a finite set of states. If there is also a finite set of possible input signals and a finite set of outputs and the automaton is deterministic, it can be specified by listing, for each state, the effect of each of the inputs. The effects of an input are twofold — it may produce an output and it will usually cause a change of state of the automaton.

The specification of an automaton[9] thus consists of five parts. The first three are lists of the set of states, and of the inputs and outputs. There is also a *Cartesian mapping* of states × inputs into states, and a similar mapping of states × inputs into outputs.

Suppose an automaton receives as inputs single binary digits (0 or 1) and gives an output of a 1-digit every time three 1-digits have been received as input without an intervening 0-digit. After a 1-digit has been given out, the count of inputs is returned to zero, so that a further three 1-digits must be received to produce another output. An automaton to behave in this way must have four states, corresponding to counts of 0, 1, 2 and 3 inputs of 1-digits

A *Cartesian mapping* is simply the mapping that can be represented by a table, having an entry for every possible pairing of a state and an input. The mapping indicating the next state for the counting automaton as described would be:

		Input	
		0	1
	1	1	2
Current	2	1	3
state	3	1	4
	4	1	1

where the automaton must start in state 1.

The mapping determining the output must be as follows:

		Input	
		0	1
Current	1	—	—
	2	—	—
state	3	—	—
	4	—	1

where a dash means "no output".

Although a computer program is a finite automaton, this is often not the most useful way to think of it. The number of states of the automaton will usually be an inconceivably large number, since a new state is entered whenever one binary digit in one data word is altered. (Some remarks about large numbers are made in introducing the idea of the *combinatorial explosion* in Chapter 2.)

In order to investigate some questions about what can and what cannot be computed, it has proved useful to consider a special type of computer termed a *Turing machine.* Practical computers are not built as Turing machines, but it seems to be true that anything that can be computed by a Turing machine can be computed by any other computer with enough storage space, and vice versa. Since the Turing machine paradigm lends itself to theoretical treatment, it is convenient to equate "computability" with "Turing-machine computability".

A Turing machine embodies a finite automaton, but the number of states it must have is vastly reduced by making a provision for information storage outside it. The automaton is considered to be connected to a reading and writing head which can put symbols on to a tape and can read them back from it. Symbols read from the tape become inputs to the finite automaton. Each output of the automaton is a combination of a symbol to be placed on the tape at the current position of the read-write head and an instruction to move the tape forward or back.

The external information storage, provided by the tape, allows a much simpler automaton than would be needed to do the same thing without the tape. It also means that a Turing machine is not limited to any fixed amount of store, since the tape is assumed infinite. The separation of the data (stored on the tape) from the program and the facilities needed to run it (represented by the finite automaton) fits with how computation is usually viewed. Practical computers do not have unlimited storage, but modern ones have a very large amount of it. Since the purpose of the Turing machine is to allow study of what is computable *in principle* it is useful to let it be able to call on infinite storage.

To see how a Turing machine can operate, suppose the tape can carry, in any location on it, one binary digit (i.e. either 0 or 1). Suppose a number n (positive non-zero integer) is represented on the tape by a sequence of n 1-digits, bounded in both directions by 0-digits. Then a Turing machine to subtract unity from a given number can be made as follows. It will be assumed that the read-write head is initially positioned on the leftmost 1-digit in the sequence (though in fact it could be any 1-digit in it for this particular purpose).

The automaton must cause the head to move to the right (it is convenient to speak of the head moving rather than the tape) until it encounters a 0-digit. It must then step back one place and write a 0-digit, thus obliterating one of the 1-digits. The automaton must have two states, of which State 1 is that in which it starts and in which it remains when the head is moved to the right and encounters another 1-digit. State 2 is entered when a move to the right brings the head to a 0-digit. Following the step back and the writing of a 0-digit where there was previously a 1-digit there is no indication of a new state; instead the command H for "halt" appears.

The state transitions of the finite automaton are determined by the mapping:

		Input 0	1
Current	1	2	1
state	2	—	H

The outputs of the automaton are as follows, each consisting of a symbol to be written on the tape (being what is already on it for the entries in the upper line of the table) and an indicator for a move of the head to left or to right. The lower-left entry would never be reached, and the lower right one has no indicator for a move because the automaton halts:

| | | Input | |
		0	1
Current	1	0L	1R
state	2	—	0

This is of course a very simple example of a computation to be performed by a Turing machine.

The theoretical treatment of computability, made possible by the Turing-machine paradigm of the computing process (or other equivalent ones) is important in A.I. since it shows there is no algorithmic solution to certain of the problems treated in A.I. by heuristic methods (see next chapter). Most people's intuition does not lead them to expect an algorithmic solution, but it is useful to have the matter firmly settled.

The representation of programs as finite automata or as Turing machines is, of course, completely formal, with no mention of ideas like "goals" or "learning" or "strategy". In the rest of this book programs tend to be discussed in these informal, purpose-related terms. It is important to remember that quite different representations of a system are possible, and that attempts to understand natural intelligence depend on representing its phenomena in some way that seems appropriate to the observer but has no absolute validity.

Appendix 1.2

PSEUDO-RANDOM NUMBER GENERATORS

The function of a pseudo-random number generator (p.r.n.g.) is to produce a sequence of numbers having an appearance of randomness, and in fact passing certain statistical tests of randomness. All of the main methods produce sequences of integers in the first place, but these can readily be scaled so that the output is a sequence of fractional values, say in the range zero to one. In the running of the p.r.n.g., each integer is computed from the one before it (or, in some schemes, from two or more of its immediate predecessors).

Perhaps the best-known method of generation is the mid-squares one, originally proposed by von Neumann. Suppose each integer in the sequence is made up of $4r$ digits, where r is an integer. Usually these would be binary digits but the radix is unimportant. In this method, each integer is derived from the one before it by discarding the r least-significant digits, and the r most-significant ones, and squaring the $2r$-digit number which remains, to give the new $4r$-digit result.

The mid-squares method is never used nowadays, because the cycle length of the generated sequence depends on the starting value, and can be quite short. There are, in fact, numbers that repeat themselves when treated in the mid-squares fashion. For the 4-digit decimal number 2500,for example discarding the upper and lower parts leaves 50, which, on squaring, gives again 2500. With other starting values there can be a long sequence, however, and the method gives a feeling for the way the numbers have to be "scrambled" to give the apparent non-predictability.

The most widely-used p.r.n.g. methods are multiplicative ones. Each number is the result of multiplying the previous one by a constant. This would produce a sequence of ever-increasing values except for the fact that the multiplication is carried out in modulus arithmetic. That is to say, the number produced is not the full result of the multiplication but the remainder left on dividing the full result by a fixed value called the *modulus*. Where the successive numbers in the sequence are u_1, u_2 .... the method may be represented as follows:

$$u_{n+1} = k u_n \ (\text{mod } M)$$

in which k is the multiplier and M the modulus.

What is probably the most widely-used p.r.n.g.[10] is the multiplicative one in which:

$$k = 455{,}470{,}314 = 13^{13} \ (\text{mod } M)$$
$$M = 2^{31} - 1$$
$$0 < u_n < M$$

For this generator, every number satisfying the constraint on u_n appears in the generated cycle, so any number in this range can be the starting-point. The cycle length is therefore $2^{31} - 2$, or just over two thousand million numbers.

If the integers generated are held as binary numbers they have to be at least 31 digits long for the above method. This is not always convenient in computers with short word-lengths such as 24. The 31-digit number can then be stored in two words, but a method working within a single word may be preferred. A useful variation of the multiplication method[11] is that in which M is a power of two, say 2^h, and k is any *odd* power of 5 such that $k < M$. The starting number must be odd, and only odd numbers are generated. The cycle length is 2^{h-2}. The number of odd numbers less than M is 2^{h-1} and these fall into two distinct cycles, each of length 2^{h-2}.

Normally, for a word length of 24, the value of h would be 23 or 24, giving cycle lengths of a few millions. The method can be illustrated by considering $h = 4$ so that $M = 16$ and $k = 5$ (the only power of 5, and hence the only odd power of 5, less than 16). If the starting value is 3, the sequence is:

$$3 \quad 15 \quad 11 \quad 7 \quad 3 \quad \ldots\ldots$$

having the expected cycle length of $2^{h-2} = 4$.

Sometimes a p.r.n.g. operates according to what are termed *m-sequences*. These can be produced by a feedback shift-register[12] (but are represented slightly differently for convenient calculation in a digital computer). Fig. 1.1 shows a shift-register with feedback.

Each cell in the register holds a binary digit and in response to a shift pulse applied to all of them the digits are transferred one place to the right. The leftmost cell can accept an input, and in a feedback shift register this is computed from the contents of the cells prior to the shift. In Fig. 1.1 the input is the modulus-2 sum of the contents of the third and fifth cells. With a suitable choice of the feedback arrangement, the register cycles through $2^n - 1$ numbers before returning to its starting-point, where n is the number of cells. During such a maximal cycle the register comes to hold all possible numbers except the all-zero one,

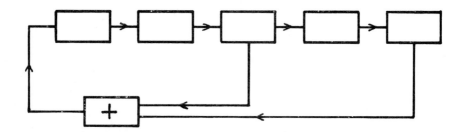

Fig. 1.1.   Five-stage binary shift-register with feedback from stages 3 and 5. The block with the plus sign represents modulus-two addition.

which is a trapping state. For the arrangement of Fig. 1.1, starting at the all-ones state, the cycle is as follows:

```
1  1  1  1  1
0  1  1  1  1
0  0  1  1  1
0  0  0  1  1
1  0  0  0  1
1  1  0  0  0
0  1  1  0  0
1  0  1  1  0
1  1  0  1  1
1  1  1  0  1
0  1  1  1  0
1  0  1  1  1
0  1  0  1  1
1  0  1  0  1
0  1  0  1  0
0  0  1  0  1
0  0  0  1  0
0  0  0  0  1
1  0  0  0  0
0  1  0  0  0
0  0  1  0  0
1  0  0  1  0
0  1  0  0  1
1  0  1  0  0
1  1  0  1  0
0  1  1  0  1
0  0  1  1  0
1  0  0  1  1
1  1  0  0  1
1  1  1  0  0
1  1  1  1  0
1  1  1  1  1
```

All of these methods generate numbers spread uniformly over a fixed interval; they are samples from a *rectangular* or *uniform* distribution. Often what is wanted is a sample from some other statistical distribution, such as the *Gaussian* or *normal* (bell-shaped "error curve") distribution, or the *negative exponential* one. Numbers which are samples from these distributions can be derived from the rectangular-distribution samples by a variety of techniques. For example, if x is a sample from a uniform distribution with range 0 to 1, $-\log x$ is a sample from a *negative exponential distribution*. If the samples from the uniform distribution are produced in batches such that the number in each batch is fairly large, say twelve, the numbers produced by summing each batch are samples from a distribution which is approximately *Gaussian*.

REFERENCES

1. A.M. Turning, "Computing machinery and intelligence" *Computers and Thought* pp. 11-35 (See Ref. 8).

2. D.R. Hofstadter, *Gödel, Escher, Bach*: *An Eternal Golden Braid* (Penguin Books, Harmondsworth, 1980).

3. N. Wiener, *Cybernetics* (Wiley, New York, 1948).

4. W.S. McCulloch, "What is a number, that a man may know it, and a man, that he may know know a number?" *General Semantics Bulletin* Nos. 26 and 27, 7-18 (1960).

5. M. Minsky, "Steps toward artificial intelligence" *Computers and Thought* pp. 406-450 (See Ref. 8).

6. J. McCarthy, "Programs with common sense" *Mechanisation of Thought Processes* (HMSO, London, 1959) pp. 75-91.

7. J.R. Slagle, *Artificial Intelligence: the Heuristic Programming Approach* (McGraw-Hill, New York, 1971).

8. E.A. Feigenbaum and J. Feldman (Ed) *Computers and Thought* (McGraw-Hill, New York, 1963).

9. M.L. Minsky, *Finite and Infinite Machines* (Prentice Hall, Englewood Cliffs, N.J., 1967).

10. A.R. Edmonds, "The generation of pseudo-random numbers on electronic digital computers" *Computer J.* **2**, 181-185 (1960).

11. A. Ralston and H.S. Wilf (Ed) *Mathematical Methods for Digital*

Computers (Wiley, New York, 1960) p. 253.

12. A.M. Andrew, "Counting to 1 099 508 482 050 without carries" *Electronic Engineering* **38**, 172-175 (1966).

Chapter 2

HEURISTICS

The word *heuristic* appears very frequently in the Artificial Intelligence literature, and denotes a very important idea. The dictionary meaning of the word (Shorter Oxford English Dictionary) is as follows:

Heuristic. Serving to find out; specifically applied to a system of education under which a pupil is trained to find out things for himself.

The word has been used in a derogatory sense by medical practitioners, a *heuristic* being to them a person who practices medicine but has acquired his know-how by experience rather than by study at an approved medical school.

The word "heuristic" is from the same Greek stem as Archimedes' famous cry of "Eureka!". There is, in fact, controversy over the correct pronunciation of the ancient Greek language and it is possible that what Archimedes actually cried out was not "Eureka!" but "Heureka!".

In the A.I. context the word *heuristic* is given a more specific meaning than that of the Shorter Oxford English Dictionary. It is contrasted with the term *algorithm*, which must first be introduced.

ALGORITHMS

An *algorithm* is a set of instructions, or an established procedure, for carrying out some operation. Long multiplication and long division are algorithms, and provided the input data on which they are made to operate are in the required form (decimal numbers, for the usual versions of these algorithms) they always produce the required result.

Algorithms need not be restricted to arithmetic. Algebraic manipulations can also be determined by precise sets of rules. For example, the solution of a set of simultaneous equations with numerical coefficients can be performed algorithmically, as can also the differentiation of an algebraic expression with respect to a variable (x, say) appearing in it. Algorithms can always be implemented as computer programs unless there is some quantitative difficulty such as insufficient storage space in the available computer.

The early stages of a person's training in mathematics tend to be fairly much concerned with algorithmic operations. Even in these early stages the student is expected to acquire skills which are essentially non-algorithmic, since facility in carrying out the algorithmic procedures is of little value unless they can be related to real-world problems. However, what may be termed the hard core of the early mathematical training is essentially algorithmic.

When the student reaches more advanced levels in mathematics he finds he is asked to do many things for which no algorithms exist. In particular, he is asked to find proofs for given statements, or theorems, and there is certainly no obvious algorithmic way of deriving a proof from the statement of what is to be proved. In fact, as will be shown shortly, there usually is a means by which, in principle, a proof could be found algorithmically if an upper limit to its length can be assumed. This algorithmic method is not feasible in practice for either a person or a machine, and certainly does not correspond to the way people do solve such problems.

Somehow, the nature of the proof he seeks must have been suggested to the student (if he is successful) by features of what he was asked to prove. These features are what are termed *heuristics* and rules employing them are *heuristic rules*. Some heuristic rules employed by mathematicians are quite simple; clearly if the statement of what is to be proved mentions, say, parallel lines, certain earlier theorems are immediately suggested as being likely to be helpful. Other heuristic rules are very subtle.

The aim of much work in Artificial Intelligence is to implement in computer programs problem-solving methods depending on heuristics. Mathematical theorem-proving is a challenging application area that has received much attention. It is an area readily accepted as "intelligent" or even "intellectual" when the activity is carried out by a human being.

Since heuristics, when employed by a human, are of the nature of "hints" or "suggestions", methods employing them do not follow an easily-predictable path to the goal, as do algorithmic methods. Heuristic methods of problem-solving are sometimes referred to as "methods which do not always work", and it is certainly true that one set of heuristics may fail to find a solution where another set will succeed.

The distinction between heuristics and algorithms has to be examined with some care, however. Some problem areas, that of theorem-proving being an example, are such that no solution method will always succeed. There is a sense in which the seeming deficiency of the heuristic method is inherent in the problem area rather than in the method.

Another complication is the fact that any computer program which invariably terminates constitutes, by definition, an algorithm. If, therefore, the claim is made that such a program operates on heuristic principles, the claim can only be sustained if the program is looked at from a particular point of view. (The restriction of attention to programs which always terminate is not very significant in practice, even though the "halting problem for automata" is important in Computability Theory. In practice, a run of a program is if necessary terminated by the computer operator, or automatically by the operating system, after what is thought to be the maximum permissible running time. Being so halted is one of the ways in which a program can fail to solve a problem.)

That computer programs can be looked at from different points of view was seen in the discussion of Finite Automata in Appendix 1 to Chapter 1. With regard to problem-solving in general a heuristic program is one which sometimes works and sometimes does not. It is, however, algorithmic in that it must behave in exactly the same way when presented with the same problem on different occasions, one of the ways in which it may respond being failure. In this consistency it differs from a human problem-solver, who has good days and bad days, and also a capacity to learn from experience (and perhaps to deteriorate as he advances in years).

A capacity for learning from experience has been built into some A.I. programs. With this capability the program can only be seen as one algorithm if its responses are seen as functions of all its history rather than merely of the inputs during the current run. Most A.I. programs, however, do not embody a capacity for learning, a fact which will receive further comment in the final chapters.

To examine some aspects of heuristic programming more closely it is necessary to introduce a distinction between two types of problem, namely problems which are and are not *well-defined*.

WELL-DEFINED AND ILL-DEFINED PROBLEMS

A problem is *well-defined* if there is some way in which a problem-solver knows, or could in principle come to know, when he has solved it. People solving well-defined problems tend to say "Yes — of course". To put it a little more formally, a *well-defined problem* is such that, given something which is purported to be a solution, an algorithmic method can be applied to determine whether it is indeed a solution.

Theorem-proving in mathematics is concerned with well-defined problems since, once a proof has been found, the checking of its validity is a relatively simple matter and algorithmic. A familiar example of a well-defined problem requiring heuristics for its solution is formal integration of an algebraic expressions with respect to one of its variables, say x. The integration process is not in general algorithmic (even though many expressions can be recognised as standard forms). However, any expression which is purported to be the integral can be checked for validity by differentiating it with respect to x. Since formal differentiation is algorithmic, it follows that formal integration is well-defined.

Most problems in everyday life are ill-defined; we select courses of action with no certainty (often, not even in retrospect) that they were the best possible in the circumstances. Perhaps somewhat surprisingly, in view of the neatly quantified nature of the input data, the selection of a move in a game of chess has to be seen as an ill-defined problem — see Chapter 5.

Well-defined problems are usually such that an algorithmic method of solution is possible in principle. At least, it is if an upper limit can be placed on the complexity of solutions which will be considered. It is then possible to define a *solution space* which must contain a true solution if there is one (within the assumed bound of complexity). For formal integration the solution space could be made to contain all possible algebraic expressions up to some assumed length; for theorem-proving it would contain all proof-like structures containing less than the assumed number of steps. Obviously the size of the solution space can be greatly reduced by very simple devices — for example, that for formal integration is much reduced if attention is given only to expressions containing the same set of variables as does the given expression, and the set of proof-like structures is reduced if all of them are required to contain only valid steps.

If a solution space can be defined, as well as an exhaustive way of exploring it, a well-defined problem can *in principle* be solved algorithmically. All that is necessary is to explore the space, applying to each of its constitutent elements the algorithmic procedure which is available to test whether this is indeed a solution. The search can be continued until a solution is found.

The snag, of course, is that the solution spaces for non-trivial problems become much too large for any method depending on exhaustive search to be feasible. The term *combinatorial explosion* is used to refer to the fact that the size of the space increases extremely steeply with increase of the number of decisions required to specify each possibility. If each decision were binary, the number of possibilities would be 2^n, where n is the number of decisions. Some feeling for the rate of growth may be obtained by reflecting that n need only be in the mid-twenties to let the number of possibilities be equal to the population of Britain, and only a little higher to equal that of the U.S.A. or the U.S.S.R. The number of ways of punching an ordinary punch card (12 rows and 80 columns) is 2^{960}, which is greater than the *cube* of Eddington's estimate of the number of particles in the Universe! (This is on the assumption that the patterns of holes in the card are unrestricted. The number of possibilities for representing alpha-numeric data according to the usual conventions is in the region of the square root of Eddington's number.)

Although the methods they allow are not implemented in search procedures as ordinarily understood, the principle of using heuristics is often explained by making reference to such a search. The finding of a solution *is* a matter of making a selection from a solution space, even if it is not very helpful to the problem-solver to describe it so. It is now possible to understand the definition given by Feigenbaum and Feldman (the correction in square brackets being mine):

"A *heuristic* (*heuristic rule, heuristic method*) is a rule of thumb, strategy, trick, simplification, or any other kind of device which drastically limits search for solutions in large problem [more correctly, solution] spaces.''

Because of the combinatorial explosion, problems can only be solved by limiting the search *very* drastically, usually to such an extent and in such a way that it does not look like a search process at all.

EXAMPLES OF HEURISTICS

Heuristics, then are general rules which guide the hopefully-intelligent system towards its goal. Many proverbs can be thought of as heuristics for everyday living, e.g. ''Honesty is the best policy'' or ''Waste not, want not''. Most people would agree that, while these are good rules to follow most of the time, they do not always ''work''. (''White lies'' can be invaluable in smoothing relationships; costs of repair and maintenance can be such that some items are best put on the scrap heap.)

Some heuristic principles which have been used, or at least proposed, can be described as ''administrative methods''. There is a need for suitable administration of the problem-solving process whenever there is a multiplicity of methods which might be followed. The administration would be such that the method judged (by some heuristic criterion) to be most promising would be tried first, but only a certain amount of computational effort would be expended on it before trying an alternative, and so on. It is also conceivable that an overall administrator could keep a watch for circular chains of deduction so as to interrupt them, and so on. The term ''administration'' immediately implies a hierarchical structure for the problem-solver, perhaps best achieved in computer systems by a special hardware provision. (Modern multi-user computers already have built-in administration of a sort, since user programs are controlled by an *operating system*. This determines the sequence of user programs, limits their running times if necessary, allocates the physical resources of the computer, and keeps accounts of the computer time chargeable to the different users.)

Minsky[1] has referred to the following essentially-administrative features of heuristic programs:
(a) Methods which set up new problems as sub-goals.
(b) Methods which set up new problems as models.
(c) Methods of characterisation or description (see discussion of the *basic learning heuristic*, below).

In order that these methods may be employed effectively, the administrative section of the program must be able to form estimates of the difficulty of sub-problems and also of their probable utility, and to use these in planning the problem-solving process.

The development of A.I. has not gone exactly as visualised in this early paper by Minsky, and most programs do not have the strongly hierarchical nature he implies. It is likely, however, that future work will follow these ideas more closely. There is a good deal of evidence that the brain embodies sub-systems which administer other sub-systems, and a similar arrangement is likely to be advantageous in any highly-versatile problem-solver.

A number of heuristic principles having an administrative flavour can be found in existing programs, however. The General Problem Solver of Newell, Shaw and Simon, shortly to be described, makes use of estimates of sub-problem difficulty. It uses them in order to avoid wasting effort on any sub-problem which seems to be more difficult than one of the problems to which it is subordinate.

Heuristics having an essentially-administrative function will also be described in connection with game-playing programs, in Chapter 5. It will be shown that the advantage gained by employing the *alpha-beta procedure* is strongly dependent on the order in which certain operations are carried out. A heuristic method is useful in determining the ordering as one which, while not necessarily optimal, is probably much better than random ordering.

As will be shown, there is a whole range of heuristics which are best discussed in connection with computer game-playing. The important heuristic principle of *means-ends analysis* and its application in the General Problem Solver are described in the next chapter. Before leaving this rapid overview of heuristics, however, mention should be made of the *Basic Learning Heuristic* of Minsky and Selfridge[2].

The *Basic Learning Heuristic* seems, at first sight, to be too obvious to be worth enunciating. It is as follows: "In a novel situation try methods like those that have worked best in similar situations".

The application of the Basic Learning Heuristic in real problem solving involves the choosing of suitable objective criteria of problem (and hence situation) similarity, and also of solution similarity. The finding of these is likely to be far from trivial.

As a model of human learning the Basic Learning Heuristic may be misleading, since it suggests that the problem-solver, faced with a problem, begins there and then to review the past occasions on which he solved similar problems. It is quite possible he does this so far as *recent* past occasions are concerned, but he is unlikely to recall the details of those in the remote past. The benefit he derives from these depends on abstractions or generalisations he made from the experience. Nevertheless the overall result must conform to the Basic Learning Heuristic, which was introduced in the course of a discussion of the inadequacy of some simple proposals for learning machines.

The idea of a measure of problem similarity, necessary in order to apply the Basic Learning Heuristic, is also discussed by Minsky[3] under the name of *heuristic connection* between problems. This is a very important idea with profound implications about the nature of intelligence, as will be shown in the final chapters.

The next four chapters, dealing with Theorem-Proving and Game Playing, will discuss ways in which heuristic methods have been put to use. Ideas which have been introduced in very general terms in the foregoing may be clarified by discussion in a practical context.

REFERENCES

1. M.L. Minsky, "Some methods of artificial intelligence and heuristic programming" *Mechanisation of Thought Processes* (HMSO, London, 1959) pp. 3-36.

2. M. Minsky and O.G. Selfridge, "Learning in random nets" in: *Information Theory* E.C. Cherry (Ed) (Butterworth, London, 1961) pp. 335-347.

3. M. Minsky, "Steps toward artificial intelligence" In: *Computers and Thought* E.A. Feigenbaum and J. Feldman (Ed) (McGraw-Hill, New York, 1963) pp. 406-450.

Chapter 3

THEOREM-PROVING

The proving of theorems in mathematics is an attractive area of application of A.I. principles, representing the achievement of a type of activity readily accepted as "intelligent" or "intellectual" when performed
by humans. There is also a sense in which it represents a natural direction in which to try to extend machine capabilities.

The first uses of computers were essentially arithmetical; Babbage's
work was largely aimed at the compilation of tables required by the Ad-
miralty, in a new way which would be both labour-saving and error-
free. It is hardly necessary to mention here that computers can be made
to do other things, but it is still true that arithmetical work constitutes
much of the work load of existing computers and provides the main
economic justification for their existence.

If required, however, computers can be programmed to manipulate
symbols and to engage in algebra and formal logic rather than arithmetic. Rather special programming techniques are required for these areas,
usually referred to by the not-very-descriptive term *list-processing* —
see Chapter 13.

Since computer capabilities have gone from arithmetic to the
manipulation of symbolic expressions, an extension to theorem-proving
seems a natural next step. It has also been seen as a good area in which
to study human problem-solving methods, and the work of Newell,
Shaw and Simon[1] culminating in the General Problem Solver was explicitly intended to model what humans were doing.

Also, there has been the belief that computer methods might break new ground in mathematics by discovering completely new theorems. This hope has not been fulfilled in any significant way, even though programs have been able to prove theorems, and to explore consequences of known theorems, in many areas of mathematics. For years the computer methods have appeared to be poised ready to make new discoveries but have not been able to claim a significant "first".

In some of the early work on theorem-proving there was the discovery of what was thought to be a new and elegant proof of the equality of the base angles of an isosceles triangle. The usual proof (Fig. 3.1) involves drawing a line AD from the vertex A to the mid-point of the side BC, or else drawing AD perpendicular to BC (AB and AC being the two equal sides of the triangle ABC). It is then shown that the triangle ABD is congruent with the triangle ACD and hence that the angles ABD and ACD are equal.

The alternative proof does not require the extra line AD. It depends on proving the congruence of the two triangles ABC and ACB, which are the same triangle with the vertices listed in different orders. These triangles are congruent because the side AB of the first equals AC of the second (because of ABC being isosceles) and similarly for AC of the first and AB of the second. Also, of course, side BC of the first equals CB of the second. The equality of the base angles follows from the congruence of these two mirror-image triangles.

This alternative proof of a well-known result has some claim to special elegance since it dispenses with the construction line AD. Strictly speaking it was not discovered during the running of a computer pro-

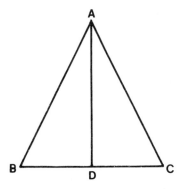

Fig. 3.1. Isosceles triangle with construction line.

gram but during the exploration by hand of what a planned program would do. Nevertheless its emergence shows that automated mathematics is indeed capable of producing new results.

Much has been made in discussion of this solitary example of innovation in machine theorem-proving. Dreyfus has pointed out that the seemingly-novel alternative proof was not in fact new; it had been discovered a very long time ago but largely forgotten. Apart from this, it would be unfortunate if over-emphasis of this particular achievement were allowed to obscure the fact that automatic theorem-proving has been applied in much more advanced areas of mathematics. The applications have been successful, in that the programs have proved theorems which tax human mathematicians, but so far all the new discoveries are still attributed to humans.

In their work on problem-solving, Newell, Shaw and Simon observed that many problem-solving situations can be represented in terms of *objects* and *operators*. In the theorem-proving context the *objects* can be algebraic expressions, or expressions in formal logic, trigonometry or whatever is the branch of mathematics in which the program is to operate. (The term *General Problem Solver* was applied because the program was written so as to be applicable in different environments. There was a core G.P.S. program, and different "interface" sections of program could match it to the different environments.)

Proving a theorem can be represented as the transformation of one *object* to match another. A set of *operators* is available, these constituting the axioms and previously-proved results on which the proof must be based. Not all of the operators are applicable to any given object — in fact, usually only a few are. When an operator is applied to an object it produces a new object. Where the requirement is to prove the equivalence of two given objects, a proof is a sequence of applications of operators which will transform one of the given objects into the other.

The same general idea can be applied in everyday problem-solving. In this, *objects* are states of the Universe, or at least, of that part of the Universe which seems to have a bearing on the problem, and *operators* are the actions the problem-solver can take to change one state into another. In introducing the G.P.S. its three originators first discuss the application of similar ideas in an everyday situation. As will be seen later, the G.P.S. method has not proved to be the most powerful method for computer theorem-proving, but it is often discussed in connection with *Robotics*. Systems under that heading are required to solve real-world problems, usually those involved in changing the locations of a set of physical objects from one pattern to another, subject to constraints on the permitted movements.

The principal heuristic used in this work is that of *means-ends analysis*.

MEANS-ENDS ANALYSIS

This is a rather fancy name for a very simple idea, but one which has far-reaching implications. It is simply the idea that the action to be taken is chosen on the basis of examination of the difference between what we have (existing state of the Universe) and what we want. This may be represented by a cycle of steps, as follows:

(i)   Examine what we have, or for theorem-proving, the state of solution reached.

(ii) Compare this with what is wanted, and if there is no difference, finish.

(iii) Ask what *operator* (or *operators*) are likely to reduce the difference.

(iv) Apply, successively until one is found to work, the operators found in (iii).

(v)   Return to (i).

In order to carry out step (iii) it is necessary to have heuristic rules which relate the available operators to the types of difference identified in step (ii).

The representation of step (iv) above is an unrealistic simplification of what has to be done. To say an operator "works" is to say that it allows a sequence of further operations which ends with success at step (ii). Thus, the success or failure of an operator may not be apparent until many more iterations of the five steps have been followed. It is necessary that the problem-solving process has a *backtrack* facility. If the sequence of operations being followed does not seem to be getting to the goal, a return is made to a point where more than one operator was available in step (iv) and not all have been tried. The process is restarted from this point using one of the hitherto-untried operators.

To let this facility operate it is necessary to have criteria which give a precise meaning to "does not seem to be getting to the goal". In practical problem-solving there is another, perhaps more serious, complication, in that the attempt to apply an operator in step (iv) usually produces new problems to be solved, and those, in turn, produce new problems, and so on. The problem-solving process must therefore be *recursive*. That is to say, it must be capable of tackling problems-within-problems, by invoking itself (for the nested problem) in the course of its own operation (on the outer problem).

Newell, Shaw and Simon illustrate the use of *means-ends analysis* in everyday life by the following monologue:
"I want to take my son to nursery school. What's the difference between what I have and what I want? One of distance. What changes distance? My automobile. My automobile won't work. What's needed to make it work? A new battery. What has new batteries? An auto repair shop. I want the repair shop to put in a new battery, but the shop doesn't know I need one. What is the difficulty? One of communication. What allows communication? A telephone .... and so on."

This sequence of thoughts in the course of problem-solving is recursive in nature. The problem of taking the son to school raises the problem of getting the car into working order, which, in turn, raises that of communicating with the repair shop. The need for backtracking frequently arises. For example, the answer to "What has new batteries?" might have been "Smith's auto shop or Brown's auto shop" and the arbitrary decision might have been made to try Smith's first. If it was then found that Smith's telephone was out of order, there would be a backtrack to the point at which the choice was made and then an attempt to telephone to Brown.

It is possible that the attempt to obtain a battery from Brown also fails, and it might then be possible to backtrack to the question "What changes distance?" to which a fuller set of answers might have been "My automobile, a taxi, an automobile borrowed from a neighbour, a helicopter".

It is easy to think of complications that might arise, such that the method of solution cannot be exactly as above, or such that it would be very inefficient if it were. A possible complication which tends to be ignored in the early work (and does not apply to theorem-proving) is uncertainty of the input information. In the child-to-nursery-school example it is unlikely the person whose thoughts are represented could be absolutely certain that a dud battery was the sole cause of his difficulties with his automobile. There may then be the consideration that, if he buys a battery and it is not the answer, he will not have enough money left to take a taxi, so it would be safer to take a taxi in the first place. The problem-solving process has extra links (such as this financial one) between the available operators.

Apart from the complications associated with uncertainty there are other possible links between operators. Some of these are associated with the reasons for failure of an operator. The problem-solving becomes much more efficient if it takes account of the fact that some reasons for failure can be common to several operators. If one operator has failed for one of these reasons, it is possible to infer immediately that the other operators linked to it in this way are not worth trying.

In our example, if the attempt to reach the school is frustrated because no auto repair shop can supply a battery, it is appropriate to backtrack to the answers to "What changes distance?" and to carry on through the operators "taxi, neighbour's automobile, helicopter". On the other hand, if the reason for failure when using the solver's own automobile is that the only road to the school has been blocked by a landslide, the reason for failure applies also to "taxi" and to "neighbour's automobile" and the only alternative left is to hire a helicopter. (It is hardly necessary to say that most fathers would backtrack to the higher-order goal, not appearing in the given monologue, of giving the son a good upbringing. He would look for ways of achieving this which did not require attendance at nursery school on that particular day.)

This kind of complication is taken into account in developments of the G.P.S. idea. Another example which has been used to illustrate it is that of a two-armed stationary robot required to pick up a particular object. Two operators available to it are "pick with right hand" and "pick with left hand". Suppose the right hand is tried first, and fails. If the reason for failure is that the object could not be reached because it was too far away or because something was in the way, it could be useful to backtrack and to try the left hand. The left limb has a different point of attachment and so has a different area accessible to it. If, however, the reason for failure was that the object was too hot to be picked up, the failure of the right hand implies that the left would fail also. (It is assumed that both hands have similar tolerance of temperature and that they are equipped with sensors which would ensure avoidance of an object too hot to be handled.) If the system embodies a representation of this link between the two operators, a failure of the right hand *for this reason* will not be followed by a futile attempt using the left hand.

THE GENERAL PROBLEM SOLVER

The G.P.S. program applies the heuristic of *means-ends analysis* to theorem-proving. The mathematical environment has some special characteristics and the cycle of operations differs from what has been described, in the following respects:

(a) When the current *object* is compared with the required one in step (ii), it often happens that more than one type of difference is found. In the G.P.S. the types of difference are ranked in an order which is meant to be according to the difficulty, on average, of removing the difference. When more than one type of difference is found, that which is higher in the ranking (i.e. is judged to be the more difficult to remove) is the one to which attention is given. It is possible that the elimination of this difference may introduce new differences of types lower in the ranking. Where the *objects* compared have a nested structure (like expressions in algebra or formal logic, which can contain sub-expressions containing in turn sub-sub-expressions and so on), a difference appearing in an outer expression takes priority over differences appearing in sub-expressions. This is clearly desirable since sub-expressions may change places within the expression when operators are applied to it, so that the sub-expressions come to be paired differently with those in the goal object.

(b) Because the number of types of difference is manageably small and so is the number of operators, what is required in step (iii) can be done very simply by referring to a *heuristic table*. As presented in the published description this is a two-dimensional table whose rows correspond to the types of difference and whose columns correspond to the different operators. A cross placed at the intersection of a row and a column indicates that the corresponding operator may be effective in removing the corresponding type of difference.

(c) The instruction "apply the operator" in step (iv) may not be a simple matter. Each operator can only transform expressions of a particular form, represented in the list of operators by an expression in the variables A, B and C. Before the operator can be applied, the object to be transformed must first be made to correspond to the appropriate input form. Establishing the correspondence requires an assignment of suitable "meanings" to A, B and C, but can also require transformation of the object by the recursive application of the whole G.P.S. method. This is another way in which the G.P.S. program operates recursively.

It is worth noting that the G.P.S. method has many heuristic features besides its embodiment of the heuristic of means-ends analysis. The choice of a set of types of difference between objects, the ranking of these according to difficulty of removal, the assumption that the more "difficult" differences should be treated first, are all heuristics. All of them have plausibility and their use is vindicated by experience, but they cannot be justified by the firm arguments which can be used in connection with steps in an algorithm.

The ranking of differences according to estimates of their difficulty of removal serves another purpose in the operation of G.P.S.. The program operates by setting up a succession of goals, some of them of the form "eliminate the difference of such-and-such type between such-and-such objects". Goals in this form have difficulty-rankings associated with them, and the operation of G.P.S. is guided by the principle that a goal is rejected if it is no easier than another to which it is subordinate. This is a principle of planning as visualised in Minsky's discussion of administrative features of heuristic programs (Chapter 2); the operation of the program is determined by difficulty estimates.

APPLICATION TO SYMBOLIC LOGIC

The principles of the G.P.S. are usually explained in a symbolic-logic environment, where it can be set to prove results like:

$$R. (- P \supset Q) \text{ is equivalent to } (QvP).R$$

In this, the minus sign is used to represent NOT, the dot AND and the small v-shaped sign is OR. The horseshoe $\supset$ means IMPLIES, and "P IMPLIES Q" is equivalent to "Q OR NOT P".

The types of differences to be found between expressions are six in number. (Some of the types have subdivisions; e.g. ΔV includes the variations $+\Delta V$ and $-\Delta V$ depending on whether the extra variable is in the expression being manipulated or in the target expression. These subdivisions are not needed for the present example.) The types are listed as follows, in decreasing order of assumed difficulty:

ΔV A variable appears in one expression and not in the other.

ΔN A variable occurs a different number of times in the two expressions.

ΔT There is a difference in the "sign" of the two, in that one begins with NOT included so as to refer to the whole expression.

ΔC There is a difference in binary connective, i.e. in the logical operator (AND, OR or IMPLIES) linking the two variables or sub-expressions.

ΔG There is a difference in grouping; e.g. $Pv(QvR)$ versus $(PvQ)vR$.

ΔP There is a position difference in the components of the two expressions; e.g. $Pv(QvR)$ versus $(QvR)vP$.

There are twelve types of operator used to change the expressions. Some of the higher-numbered types require two input objects, and when they are employed there is a search through the available objects (expressions appearing earlier in the proof) for a suitable second input. For the present example only the first six operators, or rules, are required, as follows:

$R1$ $AvB \rightarrow BvA$; $A.B \rightarrow B.A$

$R2$ $A \supset B \rightarrow -B \supset -A$

$R3$ $AvA \rightleftharpoons A$; $A.A \rightleftharpoons A$

$R4$ $Av(BvC) \rightleftharpoons (AvB)vC$; $A.(B.C) \rightleftharpoons (A.B).C$

$R5$ $AvB \rightleftharpoons -(-A. -B)$

$R6$ $A \supset B \rightleftharpoons -AvB$

The part of the *heuristic table* needed to link these rules to the set of differences is as follows:

	R1	R2	R3	R4	R5	R6
ΔV						
ΔN			X			
ΔT		X			X	X
ΔC					X	X
ΔG				X		
ΔP	X	X				

The program operates by setting up a succession of goals, some as sub-goals to others, so that there is at any point in time a nested structure of goals. The steps in proving the example given are as follows:

Given: $L1 = R.(-P \supset Q)$
Obtain: $L0 = (QvP).R$
Goal 1:   Transform $L1$ into $L0$.
          Match produces position difference (ΔP).
Goal 2:   Reduce ΔP between $L1$ and $L0$. First operator found is $R1$.
Goal 3:   Apply $R1$ to $L1$.
Goal 4:   Transform $L1$ into one of the input forms acceptable to $L1$, denoted by $C(R1)$
          Match succeeds with $A = R$
                            and $B = -P \supset Q$
          Produce new object: $L2 = (-P \supset Q).R$
Goal 5:   Transform $L2$ into $L0$.
          Match produces connective difference (ΔC) in left subexpression.
Goal 6:   Reduce ΔC between left of $L2$ and left of $L0$.
          First operator found is $R5$.
Goal 7:   Apply $R5$ to left of $L2$.
Goal 8:   Transform left of $L2$ into $C(R5)$.
          Match produces connective difference (ΔC) in left subexpression.
Goal 9:   Reduce ΔC between left of $L2$ and $C(R5)$.
          Goal rejected: difference is no easier than difference in Goal 6.
          Second operator found in Goal 6 is $R6$.
Goal 10: Apply $R6$ to left of $L2$.
Goal 11: Transform left of $L2$ into $C(R6)$.
          Match succeeds with $A = -P$ and $B = Q$
          Produce new object: $L3 = (PvQ).R$
Goal 12: Transform $L3$ into $L0$.
          Match produces position difference (ΔP) in left subexpression.
Goal 13: Reduce ΔP between left of $L3$ and left of $L0$.
          First operator found is $R1$.
Goal 14: Apply $R1$ to left of $L3$.
Goal 15: Transform left of $L3$ into $C(R1)$.
          Match succeeds with $A = P$ and $B = Q$
          Produce new object: $L4 = (QvP).R$

Goal 16: Transform $L4$ into $L0$.

Match shows $L4$ is identical with $L0$, so theorem is proved.

Finally, the essential steps of the proof can be neatly summarised. It should be emphasised that this is a simple illustrative example, and that the G.P.S. can operate much more impressively.

REFERENCES

1. A. Newell, J.C. Shaw and H. Simon, "Report on a general problem-solving program" *Proc. Int. Conf. on Information Processing* (UNESCO, Paris, 1959) pp. 256-264.

See also: A. Newell and H.A. Simon, "GPS, a program that simulates human thought" in: *Computers and Thought* E.A. Feigenbaum and J. Feldman (Ed) (McGraw-Hill, New York, 1963) pp. 279-293.

Chapter 4

THEOREM-PROVING BY ANOTHER METHOD

The General Problem Solver is particularly interesting as a model of human problem-solving. Developments of it are to be found embedded in Robotics systems, where the problem situations are closer to those of everyday life than are problems of mathematical theorem-proving. Where the requirement is specifically for mathematical theorem-proving another approach has been found to be more powerful and also more readily adaptable to different fields of mathematics. The feeling of the present writer is that the G.P.S. approach is to be preferred on the grounds of "naturalness", though other writers have taken the opposite view. The alternative approach is termed the *Resolution Method*.

THE RESOLUTION METHOD

The method operates on a set of statements, termed *clauses*, so as to derive from them further clauses. The initial clauses are devised by the user to embody the axioms of the mathematical system in which it is desired to operate and the premises on whose basis the theorem is to be proved. They also include a *denial* of what is to be proved. The advantage of including the denial rather than the assertion is that the appearance of a contradiction means the result has been proved.

The usual way to express a *clause* is as a string of elementary expressions termed *literals*, where each literal is a function of one or more arguments. It is understood that the literals in a clause are separated by the logical operator OR, but this is often omitted in writing them out.

A simple example from Slagle's[1] book will make these ideas clearer. He illustrates the use of the method to prove a theorem as instructed in the following:

"If a finger is part of a hand, a hand is part of an arm, an arm is part of a man, prove that a finger is part of a man."

One of the reasons the Resolution Method is so widely applicable is that it is permissible to introduce as many different kinds of *atomic formula* as are needed to represent the problem. An atomic formula looks like an algebraic function, and represents an assertion which is *true* or *false*. For the above theorem we need only one type of atomic formula, which will be indicated by the symbol P, representing the relationship "is part of". The formula $P(x, y)$ is *true* if x is a part of y and *false* otherwise. If we use f, h, a and m to represent respectively *finger*, *hand*, *arm* and *man*, the following are all *true*:

$$P(f, h) \qquad P(h, a) \qquad P(a, m)$$

What we are asked to prove is $P(f, m)$ and the requirement is that we include among the initial clauses the denial or converse. This is represented by $-P(f, m)$, using the minus sign to represent NOT. The term *literal* is used to refer to either an atomic formula or the negation of an atomic formula.

It is impossible to prove the theorem without introducing the axiom of the transitivity of the relationship "is part of". This can be presented as:

If $P(x, y)$ and $P(y, z)$ then $P(x, z)$ for any x, y, z.

For the purpose of automated theorem-proving it is more useful to express this as a set of *literals* combined into a *clause* by the (understood) operator OR. So instead of representing the axiom as above by the assertion that if two things are *true* a third must also be *true*, we can say that either the third is *true* or one of the first two is *false*. Formally:

$$P(x, z) \quad \text{OR} \quad -P(x, y) \quad \text{OR} \quad -P(y, z)$$

and, since the frequent repetition of OR becomes tedious it is omitted:

$$P(x, z) \qquad -P(x, y) \qquad -P(y, z)$$

It is now possible to write down the set of five clauses which must be the starting-point for the proof, as:

1. $P(x, z)$ $-P(x, y)$ $-P(y, z)$
2. $P(f, h)$
3. $P(h, a)$
4. $P(a, m)$
5. $-P(f, m)$

The symbols f, h, a and m are constants and have the same significance from clause to clause. On the other hand the symbols x, y and z appear in a clause which is true whatever new values are substituted. Substitutions are permitted for x, y and z, provided they are made throughout the clause.

The main operation on which the method depends is that of *resolving* one literal with another. It is necessary to find two literals, in different clauses, such that, by permissible substitutions, one may become the negation of the other. For example, the literal in clause 2, above, can be resolved with the second literal in clause 1. The two literals are $P(f, h)$ and $-P(x, y)$. They can be made to be negatives of each other by substituting f for x and h for y, throughout clause 1. Clause 1 then becomes:

$$P(f, z)   -P(f, h)   -P(h, z)$$

and clause 2 remains as:

$$P(f, h)$$

Since clause 2 states that $P(f, h)$ is *true*, the second literal in the modified clause 1 can be eliminated, giving the new clause:

6. $P(f, z)$ $-P(h, z)$

That the new clause was derived by resolving the second literal in clause 1 with the only one in clause 2 can be indicated at the end of the line as follows:

6. $P(f, z)$ $-P(h, z)$ r(1*b*, 2)

Further resolutions eventually produce a clause containing no literals at all, indicating *contradiction* and therefore proof of the theorem. A possible continuation of the proof is as follows:

7. $P(f, a)$ r(3, 6*b*)

8. $-P(h, m)$	$r(5, 6a)$
9. $P(x, h)$ $-P(x, f)$	$r(1c, 2)$
10. $P(h, z)$ $-P(a, z)$	$r(3, 1b)$
11. $P(h, m)$	$r(4, 10b)$
12. Contradiction	$r(8, 11)$

The clauses numbered 7 and 9 are not really needed, and it would be a simple matter to eliminate them in a final stage of "tidying" the proof. They have been included here because they would be produced if the sequence of resolutions was determined by a particular heuristic which will be described later.

In all the resolutions needed in this simple proof, one of the literals was in a 1-clause (a clause with only one literal is a 1-clause, one with two literals a 2-clause, and so on). Resolution is also possible between two literals, neither of which appears in a 1-clause. Suppose, for example, that each of the literals appears in a 3-clause, and that the 3-clauses, after substitutions to make the literals into negations of each other, are as follows:

$$A \quad B \quad \quad C$$
$$D \quad E \quad -C$$

in which A, B, D and E are literals and C is an atomic formula.

The first of these clauses shows that if C is *false*, either B or C must be *true*. The second shows that if C is *true*, either D or E must be *true*. It is therefore possible to eliminate C and to assert that one of the remaining four literals must be *true*. The new clause resulting from this resolution is:

$$A \quad B \quad D \quad E$$

The resolution of a literal in an m-clause with one in an n-clause produces a new clause which is not longer than an $(m + n - 2)$-clause. In the above example two 3-clauses appear to have produced a 4-clause, but if the literals A, B, D and E are not all different a shorter clause will result since repetition of a literal serves no purpose.

It is possible that a clause may be derived which contains a literal and its negation. Such a clause is *true* in a trivial way; it is a *tautology*. It should be eliminated from the proof as it can be of no value in making further deductions.

Apart from *resolution*, another way of generating new clauses is what is termed *factoring*. If there is a substitution which can be made throughout an *n*-clause ($n > 1$) which makes two or more of its literals identical, then all but one of the identical literals so formed can be eliminated. This leaves a clause having fewer than *n* literals. An example of a proof using *factoring* will be given later.

A MORE IMPRESSIVE EXAMPLE

The example in terms of "a finger is part of a hand" etc. introduces the general idea of the method but is, of course, a trivial example of its use. An example which may convince the reader that the method has worthwhile applications is the proof of the following theorem in abstract algebra:
"If an associative system has an identity element, and the square of every element is the identity, then the system is commutative."
The system has an operation which can be termed "multiplication" and which will be represented by a dot. If the identity element is e, it follows that:

$$e \cdot x = x \quad \text{(left identity)}$$
$$x \cdot e = x \quad \text{(right identity)}$$

for all x.
The property of *associativity* means that:

$$(x \cdot y) \cdot z = x \cdot (y \cdot z)$$

for all x, y and z.
In order to express these assertions in the required form, a type of atomic formula $P(x, y, z)$ is introduced, taking the value *true* if $x \cdot y = z$ and *false* otherwise. Then the existence of the identity element is asserted by the clauses

$$P(e, x, x) \quad \text{and} \quad P(x, e, x)$$

The representation of *associativity* in the required form is somewhat more difficult. Since the number of variables in the proof can become quite large (and also because it is often necessary to rename variables), it is convenient to use subscripted variables like $x_1, x_2, x_3 \ldots$ instead of the succession of letters x, y, $z \ldots$
The associativity property can then be represented as:

$$(x_1 \cdot x_2) \cdot x_4 = x_1 \cdot (x_2 \cdot x_4) \tag{1}$$

(The use of x_4 where x_3 might have been expected has no special significance. It leads to final expressions which look slightly more tidy than they otherwise would, with subscripts tending to follow in sequence.)

There are actually two assertions in this representation of associativity; there is the assertion that truth of the left-hand side implies truth of the right-hand side, and *vice versa*.

Now if $x_1 . x_2 = x_3$ and $x_2 . x_4 = x_5$ the l.h.s. of equation (1) is equal to $x_3 . x_4$ and its r.h.s. to $x_1 . x_5$.

If, therefore, $x_1 . x_2 = x_3$ and $x_2 . x_4 = x_5$ (as above) and $x_1 . x_5 = x_6$, equation (1) asserts that $x_3 . x_4 = x_6$.

This assertion can be put into the required form by the method previously used, to give the clause:

$$-P(x_1, x_2, x_3) \quad -P(x_2, x_4, x_5) \quad -P(x_1, x_5, x_6) \quad P(x_3, x_4, x_6)$$

Equation (1) also makes an assertion the other way round, so that if $x_1 . x_2 = x_3$ and $x_2 . x_4 = x_5$ (as above) and $x_3 . x_4 = x_6$ then $x_1 . x_5 = x_6$. This assertion, put into the required form, becomes:

$$-P(x_1, x_2, x_3) \quad -P(x_2, x_4, x_5) \quad -P(x_3, x_4, x_6) \quad P(x_1, x_5, x_6)$$

The further premise of the theorem, that the square of every element is the identity, is represented by the clause:

$$P(x_1, x_1, e)$$

What is to be proved is that the system is commutative, i.e. that $x . y$ equals $y . x$ for all x and y. The denial consists of the assertion that there are values a and b such that $a . b \neq b . a$. If $a . b = c$ this is represented by the two clauses:

$$P(a, b, c)$$
$$-P(b, a, c)$$

The starting clauses of the proof can now be assembled:

1. $P(e, x_1, x_1)$
2. $P(x_1, e, x_1)$
3. $-P(x_1, x_2, x_3) \quad -P(x_2, x_4, x_5) \quad -P(x_1, x_5, x_6) \quad P(x_3, x_4, x_6)$
4. $-P(x_1, x_2, x_3) \quad -P(x_2, x_4, x_5) \quad -P(x_3, x_4, x_6) \quad P(x_1, x_5, x_6)$
5. $P(x_1, x_1, e)$
6. $P(a, b, c)$
7. $-P(b, a, c)$

It should be noted that, while the constants a, b, c and e have the same meaning from clause to clause, the variables x_1, x_2 ... are local to the clauses in which they appear. The variable x_1 appearing in clause 1 has no connection with the variables of the same name appearing in clauses 2 to 5. When clauses are combined by resolution, therefore, it is often necessary to rename some of the variables so that they are distinguished from identically-named variables in the other clause.

A sequence of resolutions constituting a proof of the theorem will now be given, but without any attempt, at this stage, to explain why a particular resolution was chosen at any step, out of numerous possibilities.

The first step is to resolve the second literal of clause 3 with the single literal of clause 5. The variables in clause 5 are allowed to keep their old names, so the substitutions made in clause 3 must include the following:

$$x_2 \rightarrow x_1 \quad x_4 \rightarrow x_1 \quad x_5 \rightarrow e$$

Since the "old" x_1 of clause 3 cannot be allowed to keep its name, it is also necessary to make the substitution:

$$x_1 \rightarrow x_2$$

and x_3 and x_6 can retain their old names. The new clause arrived at by resolution is:

8. $-P(x_2, x_1, x_3) \quad -P(x_2, e, x_6) \quad P(x_3, x_1, x_6)$

The next step is to resolve the first literal of clause 4 with clause 5. For this, the variables of clause 5 again retain their names, and so does x_1 of clause 4. Other variables in clause 4 are renamed as follows:

$$x_2 \rightarrow x_1 \quad x_3 \rightarrow e$$

and x_4, x_5 and x_6 retain their old names. The new clause arrived at by resolution is:

9. $-P(x_1, x_4, x_5) \quad -P(e, x_4, x_6) \quad P(x_1, x_5, x_6)$

Resolution of the first literal of clause 3 with the single literal of clause 6 requires that the variables in clause 3 are replaced by constants as follows:

$$x_1 \rightarrow a \quad x_2 \rightarrow b \quad x_3 \rightarrow c$$

and the variables with higher subscript numbers retain their old names. The result is:

10. $-P(b, x_4, x_5)$ $-P(a, x_5, x_6)$ $P(c, x_4, x_6)$

Resolution of the single literal of clause 1 with the second of clause 9 requires the following renaming of variables in clause 9:

$$x_4 \rightarrow x_1 \quad x_6 \rightarrow x_1 \quad x_1 \rightarrow x_2$$

with x_5 retaining its old name. The result is:

11. $-P(x_2, x_1, x_5)$ $P(x_2, x_5, x_1)$

Resolution of the single literal of clause 2 with the second one of clause 8 requires the following renaming of the variables in clause 8:

$$x_2 \rightarrow x_1 \quad x_6 \rightarrow x_1 \quad x_1 \rightarrow x_2$$

with x_3 retaining its old name. The result is:

12. $-P(x_1, x_2, x_3)$ $P(x_3, x_2, x_1)$

The next step introduces something not seen before, as substitutions are made in *both* clauses to convert the literals to mutual negations. The single literal of clause 5 is resolved with the first literal of clause 10. For this the following substitution is needed in clause 5:

$$x_1 \rightarrow b$$

and the following in clause 10:

$$x_4 \rightarrow b \quad x_5 \rightarrow e$$

and x_6 retains its old name. The result is :

13. $-P(a, e, x_6)$ $P(c, b, x_6)$

The single literal of clause 2 is now resolved with the first of clause 13, making the following substitution in clause 2:

$$x_1 \rightarrow a$$

and the following in clause 13:

$$x_6 \rightarrow a$$

to give:

14. $P(c, b, a)$

Resolving this with the first literal of clause 11 gives:

15. $P(c, a, b)$

and resolving this with the first literal of clause 12 gives:

16. $P(b, a, c)$

and resolving this with clause 7 gives a clause of length zero, indicating:

17. Contradiction

and thus a proof of the theorem.

This example is adapted from a computer-generated proof obtained by D. Luckham, one of the pioneers of the method. The proof seems fairly complex when worked through step-by-step. The setting-up of the initial clauses (nos. 1-7) was straightforward, the main complication being associated with the cumbersome representation of associativity.

THE DISJUNCTIVE FORM

It is not always such a simple matter to translate the given statement of the problem into an equivalent set of disjunctive clauses (i.e. clauses whose constituent *literals* are linked by the logical operator OR). If it is to be claimed that the proof-finding process is automatic, attention has to be given to this part of it.

In fact, an algorithmic method has been devised which will convert a statement of the theorem in Predicate Calculus into the appropriate *clause-form equivalent* as needed.

The two examples which have been discussed were free of a difficulty which arises when the theorem contains statements including the words "for all" or others implying generality.

This difficulty arises in another example from algebra, again from Slagle, as follows:

"In any associative system which has left and right solutions s and t for all equations $s . x = y$ and $x . t = y$ there is a right identity element."

It might appear at first sight that the existence of the left sloution s would be implied by the clause:

$$P(s, x, y)$$

in which P has the same meaning as in the last example.

To give a precise meaning to this clause it is necessary to know whether s is to be treated as a constant (like f, h, a and m in the "finger is part of a hand" example), or as a variable for which any substitution may be made. It is easy to see that neither of these satisfies the requirement. Any constant value assigned to s will not hold for all possible values of x and y. On the other hand, to let s be a variable like x and y would also be incorrect, implying that *any* value assigned to s would be a solution.

The difficulty is overcome by indicating that a suitable value for s is a function of the values assigned to x and y, as follows:

$$P(g(x, y), x, y)$$

in which the function g is not specified. Functions used in this way are termed *Skolem functions*.

Similarly for the right solution:

$$P(x, h(x, y), y)$$

Associativity can be represented as before. (It is only necessary to include one of the clauses representing it, for the purpose of this example.)

What has to be proved is that there is a right identity element, which could be asserted by the clause:

$$P(x, e, x)$$

What is wanted, however, is not this assertion but its converse, i.e. the assertion that there is *no* right identity element. The simple negation:

$$- P(x, e, x)$$

is not what is wanted; it makes the assertion that there is an element such that its use as a right multiplier *never* produces the same result as multiplication by a right identity element.

To represent the required negation of an assertion it is necessary to consider right multiplication by a variable x for which any value can be substituted. Saying that x is not a right identity element is equivalent to saying that, for any value x a value k can be found such that:

$$k . x \neq k$$

Since it is only necessary to find one value of k for each value of x it is appropriate to introduce a *Skolem function*:

$$k(x) \cdot x \neq k(x)$$

or $\qquad\qquad\qquad -P(k(x), x, k(x))$

The proof is then quite short. (Clause 3 is part of the representation of associativity):

1. $P(g(x, y), x, y)$
2. $P(x, h(x, y), y)$
3. $-P(u, v, w) \quad -P(v, x, y) \quad -P(u, y, z) \quad P(w, x, z)$
4. $-P(k(x), x, k(x))$

The first step is to *factor* clause 3 by making substitutions such that its first and third literals become identical. This is done by the substitutions:

$$y \rightarrow v \qquad z \rightarrow w$$

giving

$$-P(u, v, w) \quad -P(v, x, v) \quad -P(u, v, w) \quad P(w, x, w)$$

from which a redundant literal can be removed to give:

5. $-P(u, v, w) \quad -P(v, x, v) \quad P(w, x, w)$

and then resolutions are made as follows:

6. $-P(x, z, x) \quad P(y, z, y)$ $\qquad\qquad\qquad\qquad\qquad$ r(1, 5a)

(the x of clause 5 has been renamed z to distinguish it from x of clause 1)

7. $-P(x, z, x)$ $\qquad\qquad\qquad\qquad\qquad\qquad\qquad\qquad$ r(4, 6b)
8. Contradiction $\qquad\qquad\qquad\qquad\qquad\qquad\qquad\qquad$ r(2, 7)

Although the *Skolem functions* conveniently disappear, they exert an appropriate control over what resolutions are possible.

HEURISTICS

At most of the steps in these sample proofs there were several different resolutions which might have been made. Steps which are eventually found to have been of no value can be eliminated in a retrospective "tidying" process, such as would have removed clauses 7 and 9 from the "finger is part of a hand" example. Such "tidying" can give the impression that the means of choosing the next steps is more "clever" than it really is.

However, it is essential that the means be such that the number of blind alleys followed is not too great, otherwise the time required to find a proof becomes impossibly long. The *combinatorial explosion* can strike here also.

What is needed, of course, is a set of heuristic rules which will indicate at each step which of the possible resolutions (or factorings) should be done next. The amount of computation involved in finding a proof is very strongly dependent on the heuristics used. The problem of finding good heuristics is central to implementing the Resolution Method.

One useful heuristic is the *unit preference strategy*. By a "unit" is meant a 1-clause, and when this strategy is used the next resolution will always be one involving a 1-clause so long as a novel resolution of this sort is possible. (Of course, all resolutions and factorings must be ones which have not been done before.)

Where more than one resolution with a 1-clause is possible, preference is given to those which will produce short new clauses. Thus, resolution between a 1-clause and a 2-clause (producing a new 1-clause) would take priority over a resolution between a 1-clause and a 3-clause. Also, if no resolution with a 1-clause is possible, preference is given to resolutions producing short new clauses. Thus, resolution of a 2-clause with a 2-clause (which would usually produce another 2-clause) would take priority over resolution of a 2-clause with a 3-clause. However, the preference given to unit resolutions means that a resolution of a 1-clause with even a 5-clause would take priority over either of these.

The proof given for the "finger is part of a hand" example follows the unit preference strategy exactly. At the start, the only resolutions possible are of one of the 1-clauses with the 3-clause which is no. 1. (No resolutions are possible between the negative 1-clause and any of the other 1-clauses because they all contain constants throughout.) The first resolution performed is that of the first 1-clause found in sequence, with the first suitable literal in clause 1.

Other resolutions with clause 1 are then possible, but once the 2-clause no. 6 has appeared resolutions with it take priority. The first of the 1-clauses to be resolvable with clause 6 is no. 3. When the ninth step is reached, the possibilities involving clause 6 have been exhausted, so the next two steps make use of clause 1 again.

The *unit preference strategy* embodies the principle that short resolvents are preferred. An observation which lends plausibility to this is that the desired outcome is contradiction, corresponding to the shortest clause possible, namely the null-clause.

Another heuristic found to be useful is the *set-of-support strategy*. For this the user must distinguish some of his initial clauses as *axioms*, the remainder being *set-of-support*. The rule is then that no resolutions are made between two axioms (or their factors). In the "finger is part of a hand" example the first four clauses can be distinguished as axioms, and then the first resolution has to be of clause 5 with the first literal of clause 1, so as to form:

$6'. -P(f, y) \quad -P(y, m)$

A combination of the *unit-preference strategy* and the *set-of-support* one yields a proof of this example which is one step shorter than that with unit-preference alone.

SEVERAL TYPES OF ATOM

In each of the foregoing examples only one type of *atomic formula* has been used. In the first it was $P(x, y)$, being *true* if x is a part of y. In the other examples it has been $P(x, y, z)$, being *true* if $x . y = z$.

There is no need to restrict the number of types to one. In an application in Number Theory, for example, it could be useful to have in the same proof the atomic formula $P(x)$, being *true* if x is prime, and also $D(x, y)$, being *true* if x is exactly divisible by y.

A simple example (set as a student exercise by Slagle) is the proof of the following:
"If every deceitful person is a criminal, and if anybody who encourages a criminal is a criminal, and if there is a timid person who has encouraged a deceitful person, then some criminal is timid."

The *atomic formulae* $C(x)$, $D(x)$ and $T(x)$ can be used to refer, respectively, to criminality, deceitfulness and timidity of x, and $E(x, y)$ can be another which is *true* if x has encouraged y.

That every deceitful person is a criminal is represented by the clause:

$1. -D(x) \quad C(x)$

and that anybody who encourages a criminal is a criminal by:

$2. -E(x, y) \quad -C(y) \quad C(x)$

That there is a timid person who has encouraged a deceitful person is represented by:

3. T(a)
4. D(b)
5. E(a, b)

A denial of the conclusion that "some criminal is timid" is given by:

6. $-$C(x) $-$T(x)

since this asserts that any one person is either not a criminal or not timid.

The *unit-preference strategy* suggests resolving clause 3 with the second literal in clause 6, to give:

7. $-$C(a)   r(3, 6b)

and then:

8. C(b)   r(1a, 4)
9. $-$T(b)   r(6a, 8)
10. $-$C(b)   C(a)   r(2a, 5)
11. $-$C(b)   r(7, 10b)
12. Contradiction   r(8, 11)

AUTOMATED MATHEMATICS

So far, the emphasis has been on the automation of theorem-proving, with the assumption that the enunciation of a possible theorem for proof comes from outside the theorem-proving system. Some work in this area has been aimed at producing programmes for consequence-finding rather than just theorem-proving. In other words, given a set of axioms and previously-proved results, the program finds new theorems. Such a program can be made to operate using a modification of the Resolution Method.

One difficulty in consequence-finding is in enabling the program to recognise a result which is worth reporting as a new theorem or, for that matter, one which seems to be of sufficient potential value to be worth retaining in its own work-space. Work has been done on heuristics to select "interesting" results; such results are usually capable of being expressed fairly briefly, and are not derivable in a few steps from other "interesting" results.

Work on automated mathematics has been done by Glushkov and his group in the Institute of Cybernetics in Kiev. He has suggested a computer program to be a repository for mathematical theory, probably in conjunction with a mathematics journal. Any submitted contribution could be checked by the program for both validity and novelty. This is an example of collaboration between human and machine intelligence. Such collaboration is likely to be important in future A.I. applications (see Chapter 15).

UNCONVENTIONAL METHODS OF PROOF

Not all of mathematical theory evolves in quite the orderly fashion that tends to be implicitly assumed in discussions such as the foregoing. Occasionally a proof is possible which is not entirely based on earlier results in the same area of mathematics.

Polya[2] shows, for example, that various interesting results in plane geometry can be derived by imagining shapes to be cut from cardboard and shifted around. An intriguing example of such a proof, quoted by Polya from an earlier worker, is of the following theorem:

"The area of a polygon inscribed in a circle is greater than the area of any other polygon with the same sides. (The sides are the same in length and in the order of succession.)"

The proof depends on acceptance of the *isoperimetric theorem*, as follows:

"Of all plane figures of equal perimeter, the circle has the maximum area."

The first result can be proved by supposing that the segments of area between the sides of the polygon and its circumscribed circle are cut from cardboard and can be moved to other positions. The areas are shaded in Fig. 4.1. It is also necessary to suppose that the sides of the polygon, and thus the tips of these segments, are joined by hinges in such a way that the figure can be distorted as in Fig. 4.2.

Any such distortion must lead to a reduction of the total area enclosed, since the perimeter remains equal to that of the circle. This follows from the isoperimetric theorem. However, the total area of Fig. 4.2 is made up of the new, altered, polygon plus that of the shaded segments. Since the latter has remained unchanged, the area of the altered polygon must be less than that of the polygon in Fig. 4.1, and since this applies to any distortion, the result is proved.

In fact, this proof does not break new ground in mathematics,

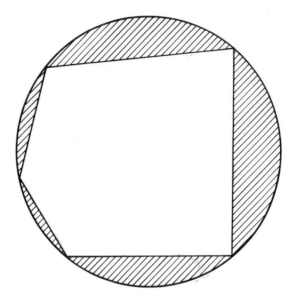

Fig. 4.1.   Polygon inscribed in a circle.

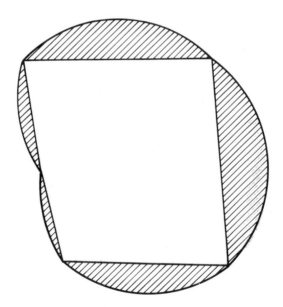

Fig. 4.2.   The polygon distorted, with the segments of circle sliding as though hinged at vertices.

because at the time it was put forward the *isoperimetric theorem* had not been proved, though it had been made to appear highly plausible. Polya gives a proof for the *isoperimetric theorem*, but it depends on proving the above result for a polygon in a different way and then deducing the *isoperimetric theorem* from it.

Despite these reservations about its ultimate value, the proof as given demonstrates that unconventional methods can sometimes be employed to prove a result in a way which people readily accept as valid. Computer theorem-proving methods would be likely to be constrained to the traditional ruler-and-compasses constructions and arguments directly supported by the axioms of Euclidean geometry. What is demonstrated here is that a human problem-solver can invoke a richer set of axioms. It can, of course, be argued that the richer set is inadmissible since a branch of mathematics should have its axioms established at the outset. At the very least, however, the unconventional methods have heuristic value; if a theorem has an ostensible "proof" using them it is likely that a legitimate one can also be found.

REFERENCES

1. J.R. Slagle, *Artificial Intelligence: the Heuristic Programming Approach* (McGraw-Hill, New York, 1971).
2. G. Polya, *Induction and Analogy in Mathematics* (**Vol. 1** of *Mathematics and Plausible Reasoning*) (Priceton University Press, Princeton, N.J. 1954) pp. 173-174.

Chapter 5

TREE SEARCH AND CHESS

In modern mathematics the word *graph* is used in a special sense. A *graph* consists of *nodes* having some particular significance, joined by lines. Each line indicates some relationship between the pair of nodes it joins. For example, the nodes might represent towns and a line joining them would indicate that these two towns are joined by a road. An ordinary map is a *graph* in this sense, but for the graph the positions of the nodes are unimportant; what is important is the pattern of interconnection.

In some applications of graphs the lines joining the nodes have the same significance in both directions. This would be true of a graph showing the road connections between towns, since long-distance routes are never one-way and the fact that town A is connected to town B implies that town B is also connected to town A. A similar representation of connectivity within a town, applicable to vehicular traffic, would be different. Many of the connections are one-way streets and the connecting lines have to be marked with arrows. A two-way street can then be represented by a pair of lines, labelled with arrows in opposite directions. A graph representing interconnections in a small town in the U.K. is shown in Fig. 5.1.

A type of graph of particular interest is a *tree*. This has one node which cannot be reached from any other, termed the *root node*. It has a set of *daughter nodes* reachable from it (two of them if the tree is a *binary tree*) and these in turn have daughter nodes reachable from

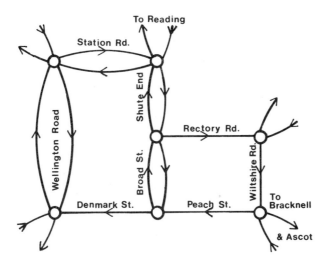

Fig. 5.1.   The principal streets in the centre of Wokingham, Berks., represented as a directed graph.

them, and so on. Any tree that can actually be drawn, or represented in computer memory, must be of finite size, so there have to be nodes without daughter nodes. These are termed *terminal nodes* or *leaves* of the tree.

Fig. 5.2 shows a tree, in which the small boxes represent nodes. Data-processing trees, unlike most real trees, are usually drawn with the root

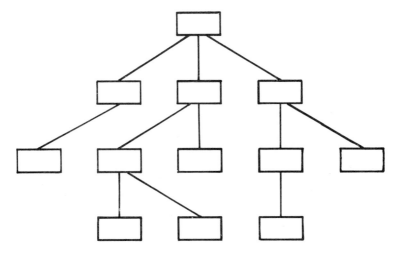

Fig. 5.2.   Tree structure.

at the top. The lines in Fig. 5.2 have not been marked with arrows even though their significance is asymmetric; the general layout indicates how the nodes are related.

There are various reasons why trees are of particular interest in computing, and especially in Artificial Intelligence. What is probably the main reason is introduced in Chapter 13 (see its Appendix 1). For the present purpose, however, the reason for interest is a different one. It is that any discrete decision process in a known deterministic environment can be represented as a tree. If the root of the tree represents the initial state of the environment, its daughters can represent the states which could result from the alternative operations which could be carried out. Then for each of these daughters a set of operations is possible, each resulting in a new state represented by a grand-daughter node, and so on.

A wide variety of problem-solving procedures, including the theorem-proving techniques of the last two chapters, can be represented as the traversing of a tree, one or more of whose leaves correspond to success in proving the theorem. Heuristics are the means of determining the choice to be made at each node, in the hope of reaching one of these leaves with much less effort than would be needed to get there by exhaustive search. For non-trivial problems exhaustive search is ruled out by the combinatorial explosion. The facility for backtracking which is an essential feature of the General Problem Solver can readily be seen as a return to an earlier node on the path so that another daughter of it can be chosen next.

Representation of these problem-solving methods as the exploration of trees is useful (see Nilsson[1]), but as has been seen they can also be discussed otherwise. (Most of the applications of graphs in mathematics are in deriving results which can also be obtained in other ways, but often the graph-theory method is the most elegant and comprehensible.)

A topic which has received a great deal of attention in Artificial Intelligence is the playing of chess and other games by computer. A type of program which has proved successful in playing a variety of games is one explicitly designed to explore the tree which represents possible continuations of the game from the current situation. This requires the introduction of a new range of heuristic principles.

CHESS

The ancient game of chess presents an obvious challenge to workers in Artificial Intelligence. There have, in fact, been attempts to build chess-playing automata prior to the advent of electronic computers. One such automaton (or what was purported to be one) was produced by von Kempelen and termed the Maelzel Chess Automaton, near the end of the 18th century. It aroused much interest among literary figures of the time, and no one was sure whether it was a genuine automaton or a box containing a dwarf or child able to play chess of a rather high standard. Edgar Allan Poe discussed this device and decided it could not be an automaton because it lost some games and won others. If it had been an automaton, he considered, it would either have won consistently or lost consistently.

Poe's argument was unsound but his conclusion correct — the "automaton" *did* contain an undersized human chess-player. A genuine chess-playing automaton was made by Torres y Quévedo in 1914. It was demonstrated in the Spanish Pavilion of the International Exhibition in Brussels in 1958. However, it only played the game from a point at which most pieces had been taken, the only ones left being the two kings plus one rook belonging to the automaton. From this point it was always able to win; there is an algorithm which can be used to force a win under these circumstances. It incorporated a turntable with a small gramophone record, and when it won a game it dropped a pick-up arm on to the record and so generated a cry of triumph.

The coming of digital computers raised the possibility of a genuine automaton to play complete chess games, and the problem of writing the necessary program was considered by Turing, Strachey and Shannon[2] (see Good[3] for a review including the more recent history).

The principle of operation suggested by each of these workers, and later embodied in successful programs, depends on examination of the tree of possible game continuations. This is referred to as the *lookahead tree*. The root node must represent the current configuration of pieces on the board, and the program is required to choose a move. In the middle of a chess game there are about thirty legal moves open to a player. The configurations resulting from these can be represented by daughter nodes of the root node.

At each of these daughter nodes about thirty responses by the opponent are possible, and the configurations resulting from these require representation in about 900 further nodes, and so on. The tree rapidly becomes very large. There are two kinds of node — those which, like the root node, represent configurations to which the program has to respond are termed *alpha nodes*. The others, representing configurations to which the opponent responds, are termed *beta nodes*. The sucessive levels of the lookahead tree are occupied alternately by *alpha* and *beta* nodes.

If the lookahead tree can be explored exhaustively, that is, to all its leaves representing all possible terminations of the game, it may be possible to choose a move which allows a machine win to be forced, no matter how the opponent responds. In fact, exhaustive search of the complete tree is quite impossible. Shannon estimated a computing time of 10^{90} years to explore the complete tree in the middle game. This was assuming a pretty fast computer, but even a speed increase by a factor of a million would leave the time at 10^{84} years — still too long to wait. The combinatorial explosion has struck with a vengeance and chess playing by exhaustive search of the lookahead tree is out of the question.

Instead of exploring the tree exhaustively, chess-playing programs explore only a small part of it. The tree may be said to be *pruned*. The simplest method of pruning is to cut off the tree at a particular depth, i.e. to look ahead some fixed number of half moves (a half move being a move by one or other of the players). This is not a very good method of playing, but even when other methods are used there is some limit on the depth to be permitted. (By "good" pruning is meant a method which gives good quality of play relative to the amount of computation expended.)

The fact that only a part of the tree is explored means that the exploration must terminate at nodes which do not represent terminations of the game. These are terminal nodes or leaves of the explored sub-tree but not of the total tree. The methods used in the programs depend on forming, for each of these nodes, a numerical estimate of the relative strengths of the two players when this configuration is reached. This estimate is made to have value zero if the sides are equally matched, or to take positive values if the machine seems to be in the stronger position, or negative if the opponent is stronger. The numerical estimate is sometimes called the *scoring polynomial* (since it usually is in the form of a polynomial or, more simply, a weighted sum) or *static evaluation function* ("static" in the sense that it is evaluated without further exploration of the tree).

Static evaluation functions have been employed by chess players since well before the days of computer chess. Where a game has had to be abandoned without hope of resuming it (in the romantic tradition of chess, this would presumably be because the enemy was at the gates of the city, or one or both of the players were about to go to the gallows), such static evaluations have been used to decide a winner.

An important component of any static evaluation function is the *material balance* or *piece advantage* term. This is simply a comparison of the pieces still held by each player, the pieces being suitably valued. There is no point in attaching values to the kings for this purpose, since the fact that the game has not ended means that both kings are still on the board. The highest value is that given to the queens, and then considerably lower ones are given to knights, bishops and rooks, and the lowest value of all is assigned to pawns.

Another component of the evaluation function is likely to be a measure of comparative *mobility*, a player being judged to be in a stronger position the greater his mobility. A simple criterion of mobility is the number of legal moves open to a player. It is also possible to make numerical estimates of *centre control* and other criteria familiar to chess players.

Having evaluated each terminal node of the explored sub-tree, the next step is to carry the results of these evaluations up through the tree ("up" being towards the root!). The method of doing this is termed *minimaxing* and it operates as follows. For alpha-nodes (representing positions from which the machine makes a move) the *greatest* value appearing in a daughter node is adopted. This is reasonable since the machine will make the move most favourable to itself. However, for beta-nodes the *least* value appearing in a daughter node is adopted, since the opponent may be assumed to make the move least favourable to the machine.

Finally, a value is assigned to the root node. Since this is an alpha node the value is the greatest one appearing in a daughter node. The move the machine then chooses is the one which transforms the existing configuration represented by the root node into that represented by the daughter node from which the value came.

This procedure can be regarded as a heuristic rule for selecting a chess move. It differs from the other heuristic rules which have been seen in that it is applied to an ill-defined problem. The problem is certainly ill-defined in practice because of the impossibility of exploring the lookahead tree exhaustively. Even if exhaustive exploration were possible it would not necessarily indicate a perfect move ensuring eventual victory. What a human player would regard as the best move is likely to be dependent on the playing strength and other characteristics of the opponent; any choice taking account of these is certainly solving an ill-defined problem. The method described above does not take any account of the characteristics of the opponent.

The operation of the method would be very simple if the tree were pruned right back until it consisted only of the root node and its daughters. The static evaluation function would then be applied at each daughter node, and that which contained the highest value would determine the move. It is found that a program operating in this way is easily beaten. No one has devised a form of s.e.f. which can usefully be applied so near the root node. The greater the amount of lookahead the better the play, and the less is the quality of play dependent on the exact form of the s.e.f..

A simple example of the use of a static evaluation function can be given as a method for playing the simple game of noughts-and-crosses (tic-tac-toe in America). The use of lookahead and an s.e.f. for this game is rather pointless except as an illustration since there are other, simpler algorithms for unbeatable play. However, it is pointed out by Nilsson that an s.e.f. calculated as follows can be used in a program to play noughts-and-crosses. It will be assumed that the machine is playing X and the opponent O.

If the configuration to be evaluated has three X's in a row (machine win) the s.e.f. takes a high value, say $+10$. If there are three O's in a row it takes a low value, say -10. (The situation where it contains winning rows of both kinds must be avoided by making a check for wins at all levels of the tree and letting any winning node be a terminal node.) For configurations which do not correspond to a win for either side the s.e.f. is calculated as follows:

(The number of rows, columns and diagonals, out of the eight possible, still open to the machine, i.e. not blocked by an O) minus (The number still open to the opponent, i.e. not blocked by an X)

Fig. 5.3 shows that the use of this s.e.f. is inadequate where the tree is only of depth one, consisting of only the root node and its daughters. For each of the five moves which can be made, the s.e.f. is returned as zero. The method fails to recognise the need to make a move in the lower left-hand corner.

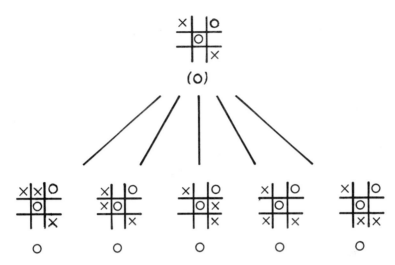

Fig. 5.3.   The unsuccessful attempt to choose a move in noughts-and-crosses by applying a simple *static evaluation function* at depth one.

Fig. 5.4 shows, however, that one further stage of lookahead ensures a correct move. Each configuration shown in these figures has beneath it a value; values not bracketted are obtained by static evaluation, and those in brackets by backing-up using the minimax method.

FORWARD PRUNING

In Figs 5.3 and 5.4 the tree is pruned by cutting off at a fixed depth. It is found that a better return (in terms of quality of play) is achieved by pruning the tree differently. Some of the pruning methods are referred to as *forward pruning*, since the decisions are taken while working outwards from the root node.

One technique for forward pruning is the recognition of what have been termed *dead* or *quiescent* positions, the others being *live* or *turbulent*. A node is more likely to be made a terminal node if the configuration it represents is classed as *dead*, than otherwise. The classification of positions as *alive* or *dead* is made by heuristic rules, the general idea being that a position is *live* if a significant change is imminent, and in particular if pieces are in danger of being taken. (The discussion is now back in a chess or draughts context.)

Another technique is *plausible move selection*. It is obvious that the tree proliferates extremely rapidly when all of the thirty-or-so legal moves from a position are represented (so that the *branching factor* is about 30). Many of these moves are ones which a human would promptly dismiss as "pointless". If the branching factor could be reduced by restricting the number of moves considered from each configuration, the proliferation of the tree becomes much less. For a given amount of computing effort this allows search to a greater depth. It is,

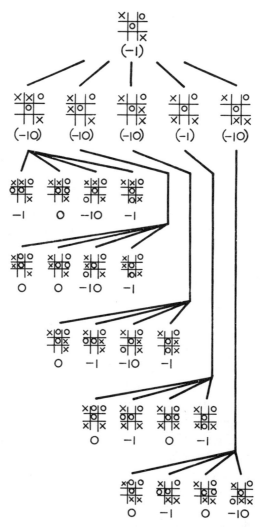

Fig. 5.4.   The choice of a move in noughts-and-crosses by applying the *static evaluation function* at depth two.

however, important to choose the moves to be those which are, in some sense, plausible, so there is interest in *plausible move generators* within chess-playing programs.

A simple *plausible move generator* can be implemented by arranging that, for all the thirty-or-so legal moves, the resulting configurations are all evaluated using the static evaluation function, and the moves to be represented in the tree are restricted to some fixed number, say seven. These are selected to be the most high-scoring ones for an alpha node, or the lowest-scoring for a beta node.

BACKWARD PRUNING

When forward pruning by any of these methods is employed, it is impossible to be sure that the outcome of the search is what it would have been if the tree had not been pruned. In contrast, the method of pruning sometimes termed *backward pruning* can be used with the assurance that the outcome of the search is not affected. A more usual term for *backward pruning* is *alpha-beta technique*, due to the necessity to refer to alpha and beta nodes in explaining it.

Tree-search, as described here, has involved two stage — the development of the lookahead tree, followed by the assignment of numerical values to the terminal nodes using the static evaluation function, and then the minimax backup procedure. The alpha-beta technique requires these two stages to be combined, so that evaluations are associated with the nodes while the tree is still being formed. Because of the nature of the minimax procedure it is then possible to omit the development of whole sections of the tree, sometimes reducing computing time by orders of magnitude.

The most natural way to think of the growth of a tree is probably as a swelling outward from the root node, so that the daughters of it are all formed, then all the grand-daughters, and so on. The development of the tree in this way is called *breadth-first search*. In order to benefit from the alpha-beta technique the tree must be developed differently, by the method of *depth-first search*. In this, the choice of which new node to form at any stage is made so that the new node is a daughter of the most newly-formed node which is possible.

To see how this can work, consider the tree represented in Fig. 5.4, which is re-drawn in Fig. 5.5 with the nodes, other than the root node, numbered in the order in which they would be developed in breadth-first search. (Strictly, it is *an* order rather than *the* order, since the order of development of the daughters of a given node is arbitrary.)

In depth-first search, with the same order of development of the daughters of each node, the first new node would be no. 1. However, the next would not be no. 2, but a daughter of the most recently-formed node, so would be no. 6. Then the next node would be expected to be a

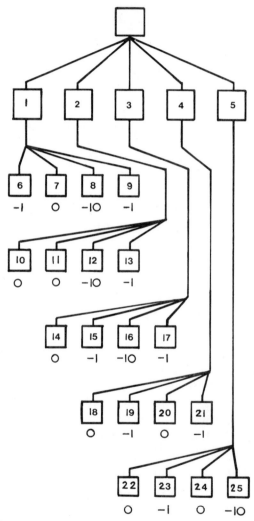

Fig. 5.5.   The tree of Fig. 5.4 with the nodes numbered in order of generation in a depth-first search.

daughter of node 6, but it cannot be because node 6 satisfies the condition for termination. The other daughters of node 1, namely nos. 7, 8 and 9, are formed before return is made to the interrupted generation of the daughters of the root node (and if node 7 had not satisfied the criterion for termination, all of the sub-tree beneath it would have been developed before node 8 was generated).

To employ the alpha-beta technique to make savings in the search it is necessary to evaluate every terminal node as soon as it is formed. A node which is not a terminal node can only be evaluated once all its daughter nodes have been evaluated. However, as soon as one of the daughter nodes has been evaluated a *provisional backed-up value* can be associated with the parent node. If the parent node is an alpha node, its p.b.v. is equal to the greatest of the evaluations so far made for daughter nodes. Conversely, if the parent node is a beta node its p.b.v. is equal to the least of the evaluations so far made for daughter nodes. Once a p.b.v. is assigned to an alpha node, it can only increase in value as the tree is further developed. Once a p.b.v. is assigned to a beta node, it can only fall in value subsequently.

These last two rules make is possible to decide, during the development of the tree in the depth-first manner, that certain nodes not yet developed cannot possibly influence the final outcome. *Backward pruning* is then simply a matter of refraining from developing these nodes. If these nodes are not ones which would have been terminal ones, the sub-trees beneath them are effectively pruned away, so the saving in computational effort can be substantial.

In evaluating the tree of Fig. 5.5 in accordance with these ideas, it would be necessary to form and evaluate nodes 6, 7, 8 and 9 in order to evaluate node 1 with the value -10, which then becomes also the *provisional backed-up value* of the root node. Then node 2 would be formed, followed by nodes 10, 11 and 12. After the evaluation of node 12 the p.b.v. of node 2 would be -10, equal to that of the root node. It is now clear that the value of node 2 will be -10 or less, since it is a beta node and its p.b.v. can only decrease. The value of node 2 cannot therefore affect the value of the root node (since it is an alpha node and its value cannot fall below its present p.b.v. of -10). There is therefore no point in continuing the development of the sub-tree below node 2, so node 13 would not be formed.

It is possible to make the general rule that, if the p.b.v. of a beta node becomes less than or equal to the p.b.v. of its parent alpha node, there is no need to make further development of the sub-tree beneath the beta node. When this happens, the search process has made an *alpha cut-off*.

The converse rule also holds, and allows savings due to a *beta cut-off*. If the p.b.v. of an alpha node becomes greater than or equal to the p.b.v. of its parent beta node, there is no need to make further development of the sub-tree beneath the alpha node.

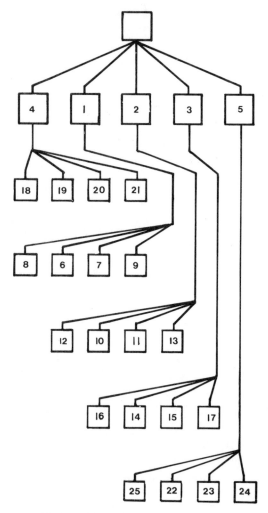

Fig. 5.6.   The same tree with the nodes rearranged to derive maximum benefit from the *alpha-beta technique*.

In the present example, after omitting to generate node 13, the search would generate node 3 and then nodes 14, 15 and 16, whereupon another alpha cut-off would allow it to omit node 17. It would then generate node 4 and all of its daughter nodes 18, 19, 20 and 21. The value of node 4 would then be -1, and the p.b.v. of the root node would rise to this figure. Then node 5 would be generated, followed by nodes 22 and 23. The p.b.v. of node 5 would then be -1, equal to that of the root node, and an alpha cut-off would make it unnecessary to generate nodes 24 and 25.

In a tree of greater depth is would also have been possible to demonstrate savings due to beta cut-offs. In this example the saving achieved by backward pruning was not very great; it was only a matter of not having to evaluate nodes 13, 17, 24 and 25. It has to be remembered that these need not have been terminal nodes and sub-trees beneath them would have been pruned out.

The amount of the saving depends on the order in which the daughters of each particular node are developed. If the order had been that indicated by left-to-right priority in Fig. 5.6 the saving would have been much greater. There would then be no need to generate nodes 6, 7, 9, 10, 11, 13, 14, 15, 17, 22, 23 or 24.

To make the most of the alpha-beta technique it is well worth while introducing heuristic methods of ordering the development of nodes. One useful heuristic is to use the *static evaluation function* to order the daughters of a particular node, the ordering giving priority to high s.e.f. values for daughters of an alpha node, and to low s.e.f. values for daughters of a beta node. Much attention has been given to the development of efficient search strategies depending on heuristic ordering and the alpha-beta technique, and more powerful ones than the above have been devised (see Nilsson).

OTHER METHODS FOR CHESS

The standard of play of computer programs for chess has gradually been improved and is now at a very high level. Programs are now in existence which present a worth-while challenge to chess masters, and generally make short work of any opponent who has not taken chess sufficiently seriously to engage in organised competitions. They do, however, work by the brute-force method which has been described, based on development and exploration of a lookahead tree.

Fairly certainly, this way of choosing a move does not correspond to how a human player does it. Humans are certainly not aware of making any large-scale search; there is a very limited amount expressed as "if I go there, he would ....., if I go there, I leave a piece open to attack .....", but only a few possibilities are considered. A chess master who was asked how many moves he considered before making his choice is said to have replied "Only one, the right one".

Evidence that the human decision process is unlike that of the computer programs comes from the fact that chess players can talk to each other about games, and a mass of literature on chess proves to be interesting and helpful to them. Their discussions are not in terms of search of an extensive lookahead tree; they make considerable use of such emotive terms as *attack* and *defence* and *threat*. These criteria are not easily implemented in computer programs. There is, however, a feeling among some workers in the area that further progress in computer chess is likely to come from study of human methods of play.

The former world champion, M.M. Botvinnick, has for some years maintained that computer chess is possible using human-like methods. In a recent presentation he described his method in terms of a lookahead tree, but one having a branching factor not much greater than unity. In other words, he claims to have a set of heuristics which usually indicates a unique "next move".

Michie[4] has also indicated an approach to computer chess which has arguably greater correspondence to human methods. At present he has given attention to the end game, where the situation is simplified by having fewer pieces on the board. When the number has been sufficiently reduced the play situations can be classified according to the set of remaining pieces, the number of classes being small enough to be manageable. For each of the classes a set of relevant "questions" about the configuration on the board is listed. The questions are readily expressible in natural language, but are also readily "answered" within the program. They are questions of the type "Are such-and-such pieces in the same row (or column, or diagonal)?", or "Is such-and-such a piece safe?". The replies are related to an indication for a move by a table look-up similar to the use of the *heuristic table* in the General Problem Solver. Although Michie is not restricted to the simple end-game situation allowed for by Torrès y Quévedo, the approach is of limited application at present.

During the history of A.I. various workers, including Ashby[5], have pointed to chess as a kind of paradigm problem for the study of human thought processes. The difficulty of imitating human methods confirms the view that something deep and little-understood is involved. It has also been argued in other quarters that chess is not the ideal paradigm problem because it is atypical of most of human problem-solving. It requires methods of thought which differ from those of everyday life in the same way as Number Theory differs from the use of numbers for most practical purposes. (Number Theory is much concerned with exact divisibility, so that, for example, the prime number 23 is a very different thing from its neighbour 24 which is decomposable into small factors.)

Partly because of this view, there has in recent years been less attention to computer chess as a means of elucidating the nature of intelligence in general, though work on it has continued for its own sake. If the current interest in simulating human playing methods bears fruit, computer chess may yet play something of the "spearhead" role envisaged by Ashby and others, at least in elucidating the nature of intelligence in a particular type of context.

REFERENCES

1. N.J. Nilsson, *Problem-Solving Methods in Artificial Intelligence* (McGraw-Hill, New York, 1971).

2. C.E. Shannon, "Programming a computer for playing chess" *Phil. Mag.* Ser. 7, **41**, 256-275 (1950).

3. I.J. Good, "A five-year plan for automatic chess" In: *Machine Intelligence 2* E. Dale and D. Michie (Ed) (Oliver and Boyd, Edinburgh, 1968) pp. 89-118.

4. D. Michie, "An advice-taking system for computer chess" *Computer Bulletin* **Ser. 2**, No. 10, 12-14 (1976).

5. W.R. Ashby, "The next ten years" in: *Computer and Information Sciences* J.T. Tou and R.H. Wilcox (Ed) (Spartan Books, Washington, 1964) pp. 2-11.

Chapter 6

OTHER GAMES

Chess is by no means the only game which has received the attention of workers in Artificial Intelligence. In fact, many little-known games have been brought out of obscurity to become the subject of an A.I. study, either because they were thought to pose problems of a suitable level of difficulty or to illuminate special aspects of game-playing.

Most of the games which have been studied are much simpler than chess. This is hardly surprising since most of the games there are are simpler than it. There is, however, also the game of *Go* which is considered to be more difficult than chess, both for human players and computers. Like chess it is an ancient game, said to have been played in the Orient for four thousand years and to be still the national pastime of Japan.

CHECKERS (DRAUGHTS)

The most famous work on a game other than chess is that of Samuel[1] on a program to play draughts, or as it is termed in America (and hence by Samuel), checkers. The game is much simpler than chess, having, according to Shannon's calculations, a number of possible playing situations which is roughly the cube root of the number possible in chess. (For chess, Shannon arrives at 10^{43} for this number. Good discusses this estimate and decides it is probably right within a factor of a thousand, but points out that many of the positions are highly improbable. He suggests 10^{24} as an estimate of the number of chess positions which are not of vanishingly-small probability.)

Samuel's main aim in his work on computer game-playing was not game-playing for its own sake. He wanted to explore ways of incorporating in computer programs the capability of improving their own performance by experience, or in other words, of learning a skill. He thought it better to work on checkers than to tackle the complexities of chess in case these obscured the primary issue.

The general method used for checker-playing is essentially the same as that of the main approach to chess-playing, relying on exploration of a lookahead tree. Two forms of learning have been embodied by Samuel, termed by him *rote learning* and *generalisation*.

Rote learning is the less interesting and less powerful of the two. It depends on storing in the computer memory a large number of board configurations which have arisen in the course of play. They are configurations which actually existed and were therefore represented in the root node of the tree (as distinct from the hypothetical configurations represented elsewhere in it).

Along with each stored configuration there was also stored its numerical evaluation. This is the evaluation obtained by developing the tree, applying the static evaluation function at the terminal nodes, and backing-up using the minimax procedure. This evaluation is, in general, different from that obtained by applying the static evaluation function directly, and is more useful in determining play.

Once a set of configurations, with evaluations, has been stored, the program, as it operates, tests for a match between the configuration corresponding to any node of the tree and configurations in the stored list. If a match is found, the stored evaluation is transferred to the node, and there is no need to develop any sub-tree which would have appeared beneath the node.

The obvious advantage of rote learning is in saving computing time, since it obviates the need to develop some sub-trees. This is another form of forward pruning. There is, however, a trade-off between computing time and quality of play since the size of the tree as a whole is limited by the time which can be allowed. Hence rote learning can either save time or can achieve better play in the same time by letting the pruned tree go a little deeper.

There is another way in which the use of rote learning improves the quality of play. When a match is found between a node and a configuration in the stored list, the evaluation which is transferred is one which was formed when the configuration was in the root node and had the whole of the lookahead tree beneath it. It is therefore an evaluation based on a larger tree than would be formed beneath the node if no match were found. Although rote learning is a form of pruning as far as computational effort is concerned, its effect on the result of the search is as though the branches of the tree where it is effective are made to sprout further than they otherwise would.

There is of course an upper limit to the size of list which can be accommodated and utilised. Not all of the configurations arising in play can be stored, and it is important to try to ensure the list is not cluttered with ones which hardly ever occur. Samuel achieved this by arranging that every entry in the list had associated with it a count of the number of moves since the entry was last utilised. If a large amount of play had elapsed since the entry last served any purpose it was culled from the list and another, from the current game, substituted. The list then came to hold a set of configurations which arose reasonably frequently during play.

Samuel found that rote learning was worth while in a checker-playing program, but it is generally agreed it has no place in chess programs. The enormously greater number of possible configurations means that a correspondingly longer list would be needed to be of any value, and the overheads mean it would not be worth while.

The other learning principle used by Samuel was what he termed *generalisation*. It allows the program to improve its own static evaluation function as it plays.

The s.e.f. is usually a polynomial, and in its simplest form is a first-degree polynomial or weighted sum, say s, computed as follows:

$$s = k_1a_1 + k_2a_2 + k_3a_3 + \ldots.$$

in which a_1, a_2, etc. are the values of the various computed criteria such as *material balance, mobility, centre control* and so on. These are weighted with respect to each other by the coefficients k_1, k_2 ..... The polynomial can also be of higher degree in the a-variable, as:

$$s = k_1a_1 + k_2a_2 + k_{1.1}a_1{}^2 + k_{1.2}a_1a_2 + \ldots.$$

but it is only necessary to consider the first-degree case to illustrate the method.

Good play depends on a suitable allocation of values to the coefficients k_1, k_2 ... , and *generalisation* provides a means of "trimming" these for improvement. The method is an example of optimisation by what is often termed *hill-climbing*. That is to say, there is an initial assignment of values to k_1, k_2 .... and at any point in time they define an *operating point*. The operating point moves through its multi-dimensional space as the k-values are adjusted, searching for a location which optimises some response or *objective function*. The term hill-climbing is used because a climber similarly alters his position in two dimensions (latitude and longitude) to maximise his height.

One possible technique for hill-climbing would be to let the program play a number of games against an opponent with the k-values set in a particular way, and then to play some further games with an experimental change in the operating point. The experimental change might be to increase the value of k_1 by a small amount. If the program wins more games in the second set than in the first, the new value of k_1 is adopted, otherwise k_1 returns to its old value, and some other experimental change is tried next.

It is obvious that any method of adjustment depending on the outcomes of complete games must make progress very slowly if it makes it at all. Since the opponent probably does not play with absolute consistency it is necessary that the two sets of games be large, but this brings its own difficulties. It is much more satisfactory if a means can be found of adjusting the k-values during the running of a single game, and Samuel devised a way of doing so.

The method depends on the observation that the quality of play of a program improves with increase in depth of lookahead. Also, the performance becomes less dependent on the exact form of the static evaluation function, the greater the depth of lookahead. These observations indicate that the evaluation of a configuration obtained by backing-up from the lookahead tree is in some sense a "better" evaluation than that obtained by applying the s.e.f. directly.

If a means of computing the s.e.f. could be found giving perfect agreement between the backed-up value for every configuration and the result of applying the s.e.f. directly to the same configuration, the evaluation must be equivalent to the exploration of an exhaustive tree. What the generalisation method does is to adjust the k-values to improve the correspondence between the result of applying the s.e.f. directly and the result of using the same s.e.f. but backing-up through the lookahead tree.

If s is the result of direct evaluation of the s.e.f., and s_b the result of backing-up, the difference can be seen as an error in s, say e, where:

$$e = s - s_b$$

What Samuel did was to make his program compute running measures of correlation between e and a_1, a_2, etc.. A positive correlation between e and any of the a_i indicates that the corresponding k_i could profitably be reduced, and conversely a negative correlation indicates it should be increased. The principle is essentially what Donaldson[2] calls "error decorrelation".

The details of the method required considerable development to ensure stability; it is easy to arrive at arrangements which produce endless "hunting" near an optimum. The final method, in fact, departs somewhat from the gradual convergence of a hill-climbing procedure and makes a rather drastic reassignment of the k-values after each move.

Despite what was said about the advantage to be expected if the result of applying the s.e.f. directly can be made to agree with the backed-up value, it is not necessarily true that such agreement produces good play. Perfect agreement could be achieved by setting all the k-values to zero, but this would clearly be of no value for playing the game. In fact, for any set of k-values which produce good play it would be possible to reverse all the signs to get very poor (in fact, "giveaway") play. However, the agreement between the two evaluations would be just as good with the negated values as with the original ones.

Samuel realised that his method could arrive at states which gave good agreement but poor play. To avoid this he arranged that the co-efficient of one of the terms in the s.e.f. was fixed at a positive value, say unity, the others being still adjustable. The term which was singled out was the *material balance* one since it is safe to assume that it is always advantageous for a player to retain his pieces on the board.

(It is worth noting, parenthetically, that this illustrates a comment made by Oliver Selfridge with reference to the Artificial Intelligence field in general. Humans come to tasks such as chess with a set of attitudes and abilities accumulated over the years. It is hardly necessary to tell a human that he should try to keep his own pieces and to capture those of his opponent; the general idea came to him when he squabbled over toys with playmates at an early age. However, a machine has to be "told" by setting the coefficient of the piece-advantage term to a positive value.)

With the *material balance* coefficient, say k_1, set to unity, the expression for the static evaluation function becomes:

$$s = a_1 + k_2a_2 + k_3a_3 + \ldots.$$

Generalisation, then, has been described as a means of adjusting numerical parameters. It is possible to use this adjustment to determine a choice of terms to be included in the static evaluation function. Samuel provided his program with a larger "menu" of criteria (a_1, a_2, etc.) than the number which were allowed to be operational in the s.e.f. at any one time. The set which was operational was altered in a straightforward way — if any k-value remained close to zero for a sufficient time, the term to which it belonged was removed from the operational set and another was transferred from the stand-by set to take its place. The removed term would be added to the stand-by set and re-introduced to the operational set for another "trial" later.

With the facility of altering the set of terms the learning method takes on a new character. It begins to be seen as something which could be termed a *self-organizing system*. Where the action is merely to adjust parameters this term does not seem appropriate; the weaker term *self-optimising* would then be applied. The distinction cannot be a rigid one, since there is no essential difference between forming a new connection (a structural change) and turning a gain setting from zero to a finite value (a parameter change). There is, however, a difference in how the system is most readily described.

The generalisation learning method was shown by Samuel to be effective. He organised the program so that it could play against itself overnight, behaving as two players *alpha* and *beta* (no connection being intended with the use of these letters to indicate types of nodes). Player *alpha* allowed modification of his s.e.f. by generalisation, while player *beta* used a fixed s.e.f.. When *alpha* won a game, the s.e.f. as it existed in *alpha* was copied into *beta*. On the other hand, if *beta* won three successive games the s.e.f. of *beta* was copied into *alpha*. This allowed *alpha* to recover if the adjustment process somehow ran amok.

Although these two forms of learning have been shown to be effective, they certainly fall far short of human capabilities. Although the s.e.f. is modified by *generalisation*, it remains a combination of criteria devised and programmed by Dr. Samuel. Although it is difficult to define the deficiency in precise terms, there is a sense in which the new versions of the s.e.f. are not qualitatively new. Samuel himself was well aware of this deficiency and gave much thought to it. It will be discussed further in later chapters.

Another deficiency of these learning methods is that they do not allow the program to adapt to the playing strength or playing habits of the opponent (unless in a very indirect way, resulting from the influence of the opponent's behaviour on the selection of board configurations actually experienced). Neither do they allow it to learn by copying the opponent. Some studies aimed at developing more comprehensive learning methods have been made in connection with other board games.

NOUGHTS-AND-CROSSES TYPE GAMES

The familiar child's game of noughts-and-crosses or tic-tac-toe has already been mentioned, and presents no serious challenge for computer game-playing. It is, however, the simplest case of a class of games played on boards ruled off into cells, with two or more players inserting tokens of respective kinds into unoccupied cells.

A variant of noughts-and-crosses can be played on a three-dimensional grid instead of the usual two-dimensional one. The length of each line is then usually increased to four cells. It is even possible to play in four or more dimensions, and computer programs can then be written which are very difficult for human players to beat. This is simply because people cannot visualise space of more than three dimensions.

A two-dimensional game of the type of noughts-and-crosses, but of an entirely different level of difficulty, is known as *Peggity*, *Go-Moku* or *Five-in-a-Row*. The board size is usually 19 × 19 cells (but is not critical) and the aim of each player is to be the first to get five tokens of his own kind together in a line, the permitted lines being horizontal, vertical or diagonal. The players take it in turns to insert one token.

It is not quite correct to lump together the games indicated by the three names. In *Go-Moku* the requirement for a win, according to Murray and Elcock[3], is to have five *and only five* tokens of the same type together in a row — a row of six does not count. For *Peggity* and *Five-in-a-Row* the requirement is usually stated as that of placing five in a line, whether or not the five are also part of a longer line. It has been found in practice (by St. Quinton) that the distinction is not important. In a very large number of games played according to the *Peggity* rules, it was found that lines of more than five tokens were never formed.

Most of the games were between human subjects and a computer program, but also a number were played between humans. (The fact that no lines of six or more were actually formed does not prove that their possibility did not influence the course of play. However, the introspections of the players supported the view that it did not.)

For games of this type it is not necessary to explore a lookahead tree. Because tokens are not moved after they are placed, the development of a winning pattern can be observed locally.

It is possible to discover, for these games, patterns of tokens which are unbeatable, i.e. which can be made to lead to the winning arrangement. Even for noughts-and-crosses in its familiar form on a 3 × 3 grid, "fork" configurations are possible which ensure victory (but would only appear in games against a very naive opponent). Fig. 6.1 shows two configurations in which the player "O" has formed a "fork" which ensures him victory, even though it is the turn of "X" to play.

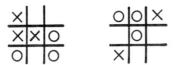

Fig. 6.1.   Situations in games of noughts-and-crosses (player "X" to play). In both situations player "O" has formed a "fork" which ensures him victory.

For *Peggity* or *Go-Moku* there are various patterns which enable a player to force a win, and successful play depends on (a) producing one of these patterns in the player's own tokens and (b) preventing the opponent producing one with his.

Murray and Elcock have written a program which learns to play *Go-Moku*. At the end of a game played against an opponent it analyses the record, backwards, to find out what patterns of tokens preceded the win. In the early stages of learning the games will mostly be won by the opponent, so the program could be said to be learning by copying the opponent. When the program has identified the unbeatable patterns it plays so as to try to achieve them for itself and to prevent the opponent forming them.

The Murray-Elcock program stores patterns in a generalised form which does not distinguish between diagonal lines and ones which are horizontal or vertical. Some such generalisation is a useful feature of a learning program, and patterns are equivalent irrespective of the angles of their constitutent lines.

A program to learn to exploit its opponent's weaknesses, however, is more powerful if it can distinguish, for some purposes, between patterns incorporating diagonal lines and those which use only horizontal and vertical ones. It has been shown that human players are much more likely to fail to recognise an unbeatable pattern when it embodies diagonal lines than when it does not, and a really "clever" learning program would come to exploit this.

The playing of *Peggity* has been studied by St. Quinton[4]. His aim was to investigate the acquisition of playing skill by human subjects, with the possibility of eventually embodying the same methods in a learning program. He asked each of his subjects to play a series of games against a computer program. Every move in every game was recorded by the same computer program, along with the time taken by the subject to decide each of his moves, and indicators for two types of signal he could initiate.

This particular game was chosen for the study as being sufficiently difficult to present a real challenge and yet sufficiently easy that many of the subjects acquired playing skill during the experimental session. Another advantage of the game is that it is not widely played (at least, not outside the Orient) and all the subjects were initially-naive players. The computer program was able to play at three different levels of strategy. In each session it started using the lowest level, moving up to the next whenever the subject had won two successive games at either of the lower levels.

Programs have been written which allow the game records to be analysed to locate the points at which significant patterns (St. Quinton calls them *keys*) arise. The subsequent development or blocking of each key can then be followed (automatically, by the analysis program) and it may be possible to infer whether the subject has, at that point, learned the significance of a key of the particular type. Learning the significance of a key need not be conscious. The study should have implications for the study of learning in a wider context. A straightforward adaptation of the analysis program could produce a playing program able to learn to profit from weaknesses of the opponent.

THE GAME OF GO

Exploration of a lookahead tree is only feasible if the number of plausible moves from a given position is not excessive. Use of the technique applicable to noughts-and-crosses-type games is only feasible if the winning pattern develops in a sub-area of limited extent. Neither of these conditions apply to the game of *Go*.

This game (see Good[5]) has a claim to be regarded as more sophisticated than chess. Certainly it is proving to be very difficult to write computer programs to play it with any degree of proficiency.

The game is played on a rectangular grid like that for *Go-Moku* or *Peggity*, and players insert tokens alternately in the same way. However, the aim is not to form a particular pattern, such as a line, of the player's own tokens. It is to surround and "take" areas filled solidly with the opponent's tokens. The "surrounding" must be such that any step out of the surrounded area, horizontally or vertically, arrives at a cell occupied by one of the surrounding tokens. The possibility of a step into an enclosed blank "island" nullifies the "surrounding".

The nature of this goal, being essentially geometrical or topological, is one for which human perceptual processes have some special aptitude which has not been emulated in computer programs. Such programs as have been written for *Go* play poorly by human standards.

GAMES OF CHANCE

All the games discussed so far have been *games of perfect information*. That is to say, nothing (except the thoughts of the opponent) is hidden from either player. These games make no use of chance effects like the throw of a die or the spin of a wheel or the cutting of a pack of cards. Games of perfect information are "trivial" from the point of view of the Games Theory of Borel and von Neumann (see Vajda[6] for a simple introduction), but the discovery of effective playing strategies is, as has been seen, far from trivial.

Computers can readily be programmed to play some games of chance. A program to play *Backgammon* has, on one occasion, actually beaten the world champion[7]. An isolated win in a game of chance is not very significant, and the computer play was judged by experts to be far from perfect.

Even where the computer cannot be used on-line, but is used to carry out analyses whose results have to be memorised by the human player, the benefit may be substantial. Slagle[8] gives an amusing account of the exploits of a professor who applied himself to the game of *blackjack* with the help of computer analysis. He amassed a substantial fortune and eventually had to disguise himself to be allowed to enter the Las Vegas casinos.

REFERENCES

1. A.L. Samuel, "Some studies in machine learning using the game of checkers" In: *Computers and Thought* E.A. Feigenbaum and J. Feldman (Ed) (McGraw-Hill, New York, 1963) pp. 71-105.

2. P.E.K. Donaldson, "Error decorrelation studies on a human operator performing a balancing task" *Medical Electronics and Biological Engineering* **2**, 393-410 (1964).

3. A.M. Murray and E.W. Elcock, "Automatic description and recognition of board positions in Go-Moku" In: *Machine Intelligence 2* E. Dale and D. Michie (Ed) (Oliver and Boyd, Edinburgh, 1968) pp. 75-88

4. J.G. St. Quinton, *Zetetics* (Ph.D. Thesis, Reading University, 1981).

5. I.J. Good, "The mystery of GO" *New Scientist* No. 427, 172-174 (Jan. 21, 1965).

6. S. Vajda, *An Introduction to Linear Programming and the Theory of Games* (Methuen, London, 1960).

7. H. Berliner, "Backgammon program beats world champ" *AISB Quarterly* (Newsletter of the Soc. for the Study of Artifical Intelligence & Simulation of Behaviour) issue 35, 9-10 (1979).

8. J.R. Slagle, *Artificial Intelligence: the Heuristic Programming Approach* (McGraw-Hill, New York, 1963) pp. 40-41.

Chapter 7

PATTERN RECOGNITION

Many of the useful things that can be done by brains but not readily by computers come under the heading of *pattern recognition*. Some of them are so readily done by humans that there is a tendency to take them for granted. When a person reads low-quality cursive handwriting, or carries on a conversation under cocktail-party conditions, he is not usually thought to be performing a highly-intellectual task. Nevertheless, he is doing something which is extremely difficult to imitate in machines. The tasks of identifying words in handwriting (or, for that matter, in printing) and of identifying words in speech, are examples of *pattern recognition*

Of course, pattern recognition need not be concerned with words; everyday living requires the recognition of people's faces as well as a whole host of objects, of which knives, forks and spoons, cabbages and motor cars are just a few that come to mind. People and animals living under primitive conditions need to be able to recognise predators and potential prey (whether animal or vegetable) and so on.

Work on artificial pattern recognition has been referred to as "providing computers with eyes and ears". As Oliver Selfridge has remarked, without pattern recognition the "intelligence" of computers has an unreal, ethereal quality. It is an esoteric type of intelligence, accessible only through textual and numerical inputs and outputs. Where the data has to be fed in by a human operator it is likely to be highly pre-selected for relevance. A computer with "eyes and ears" does not have the benefit of such pre-selection; it has to make its own selection from an enormous inflow of largely-irrelevant data, as must a person or animal.

Artificial pattern recognition brings the computer into closer contact with the real world. Work on *Robotics* allows it also to operate directly on the real world, and the two together give Artificial Intelligence a different character from that of the earlier work.

Pattern recognition may operate in any of a number of sensory modalities and need not be restricted to a single one. Visual pattern-recognition is what has received most attention. At a relatively simple level, recognition of printed characters is needed for the "reading machines" which have applications in commerce and have been developed as aids for blind people.

The automatic reading of printed characters (OCR, or Optical Character Recognition) is used commercially to a greater degree than most people realise. In most of the commercial applications the material to be read has been printed with the intention that it should be suitable for machine reading, as well as for reading by people. The reading task is greatly simplified when, as is usual in these applications, the characters to be read are all printed in one known fount. Character recognition is then essentially a matter of template-matching.

The highly-stylised characters that appear on bank cheques are well-known as an instance of printed matter intended for machine reading. They are printed in magnetic ink and are read magnetically rather than optically by the machine. This is simply because cheques tend to be rubber-stamped enthusiastically as they pass through the banking system and the numbers are likely to be inked over. Since the inks used for rubber-stamping are non-magnetic they do not interfere with magnetic reading.

These characters on cheques are designed to allow a very simple reading method. They are scanned by a vertical slit, like the recording or reading head of a tape recorder. The slit gives an output signal proportional to the amount of magnetic ink under it. The waveform of this signal, as the slit passes from left to right over a character, is different for each character type and so allows the machine to infer which has been scanned. The way the magnetic ink is distributed vertically is irrelevant for machine reading but important in letting the characters be readable by people. An advantage of this form of operation is that there is no need for the reading head to be precisely positioned vertically as the slit can be much longer than the height of the print.

It would have been possible, instead of using this ingenious method, to let the cheque carry two separate representations of the same information, one in magnetic ink for machine reading without regard to humans and the other in plain printing for human use. The advantage of having the same character read by man and machine is the saving in printing cost, and the elimination of any suspicion that the two representations might not correspond.

Apart from cheques, a great many commercial documents such as gas and electricity bills carry numbers which are optically machine-read when the bill is returned to the accounts office. The fount in which the numbers are printed is one specially designed to lend itself to OCR, but it is also pleasing and easily read by humans.

Machine reading becomes much more difficult when the characters do not come from one known fount, and when hand-blocked ones may be included. Reading machines have been produced which will accept multi-fount and hand-blocked characters, but the reading of cursive handwriting by machine is very difficult to achieve. The problem of *segmentation*, i.e. of deciding where one letter ends and another begins, proves to be very difficult.

For printed and hand-blocked characters, techniques have been developed which allow machine reading with low error rates. (Strictly, there is often both an error-rate and a failure-rate since the machine is able to indicate "don't know" as an alternative to recognition of a character.) Work has been done by the British Post Office towards the automatic recognition of postcodes and hence automatic sorting of mail. For this purpose it is not too serious if the machine indicates "don't know" for a small proportion of the mail; it only means that this proportion has to be hand-sorted along with the items having no postcode.

In connection with commercial applications it is worth remembering that there is often an alternative to the use of reading machines (like printing the number in two forms on cheques). The Soviet Union has introduced a system of all-number postcodes, and envelopes and post cards are printed with a grid of dotted lines as shown in Fig. 7.1. The postcode can then be represented by making figures by thickening some of the lines as in Fig. 7.2. A diagram showing how each of the ten digits should be formed is printed on the flaps of envelopes as shown in Fig. 7.3.

The equipment needed to "read" postcodes in this form need only

Fig. 7.1. Grid of dotted lines to be completed with a numerical post-code, as printed on Russian envelopes.

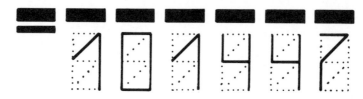

Fig. 7.2. A grid completed with the correct post-code for the Institute for Information Transmission Problems, Moscow.

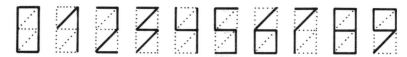

Fig. 7.3. The guide printed on the flap of the envelope to show how each digit should be formed.

position the grid correctly (aided by the heavy bars printed beside it) and then has to determine which lines have been thickened.

One of the first applications of OCR was a machine termed ERA (Electronic Reading Automaton) which was used to read cash-register slips. It was developed for a retailer having numerous branches (Boots the Chemist) and the idea was to let the data on the slips provide a record of branch transactions suitable for processing on a central computer.

An alternative would have been to fit to each cash register a device to record on magnetic or paper tape the same information as was recorded in ink on the slip. Because of the large number of cash registers in the branches it was cheaper to install one reading machine and to leave the cash registers as they were. (In practice, things were not so simple. It was necessary to give careful attention to the quality of print produced by the cash registers, to let the ERA work with the degree of accuracy demanded in commerce.)

The recognition of characters is only one facet of visual pattern recognition. Particularly as a result of interest in Robotics, the emphasis of much work is now on scene analysis rather than the older view of pattern recognition in which it was usually assumed that the image to be recognised could be presented in isolation against a plain background. In pattern recognition it is usually possible to arrange this by suitable pre-processing, but in other uses of vision it is necessary to recognise objects when they are partly obscured by other objects and are seen against complex backgrounds.

In another sensory modality, automatic speech recognition has many potential applications and has received a great deal of attention. In Science Fiction films and television series the characters usually communicate with computers in plain speech. This has the advantage of keeping the audience more closely in touch with what is happening than they would be if the computer dialogue depended on a keyboard, but it also reflects the fact that speech is the most natural form of communication for humans.

There can be no doubt that a speech recogniser, to operate without restriction on its input, is a long way in the future. It may in fact be impossible to make such a device to operate purely on the basis of the speech input. (The human speech-recognition process does not operate in isolation from the higher levels concerned with meaning.)

Where the requirement is to identify a word out of a small vocabulary of possibilities, automatic speech recognition is entirely feasible, particularly if the recognition device can be "trained" or otherwise adjusted to the particular speaker. Even a device which can only distinguish the spoken sounds of the ten numeral digits can allow a useful dialogue with a computer over a telephone link, and a facility allowing it has been added to commercial computer installations. (The generation of a spoken form of the computer output is a relatively simple matter, and has been offered commercially with a choice of male or female voice.)

A device to recognise words from a small vocabulary can be useful in many situations in which an operator has to give commands to a machine while doing something else with his hands. It can be useful for a workman to be able to call out commands from the small set "Up", "Down", "Left", "Right" and "Stop" and to have them obeyed by an overhead crane. A similar application arises in sorting postal packages, where an operator places the packages on a conveyor belt and at the same time calls out the town of destination. Without automatic speech recognition it is necessary to have another operator pressing buttons to convey the destination information to the equipment which pushes the packages from the belt into appropriate mail bags. With automatic speech recognition there is the possibility of doing without the second operator.

The late Dr. Chris Evans (National Physical Laboratory Teddington) developed a speech recognition system able to respond to a vocabulary of a few hundred words. He discussed it in the context of a system to provide information on request to the crew of an aeroplane in flight. The secret of its operation was that it was sensitive to only a small subset of the vocabulary at any one time, depending on the context. For instance, following certain questions it might ask a user, the only sensible reply might be one of the numeral digits, and in that case the system would be sensitive only to these ten words. The human recognition of speech depends strongly on context, and what Chris Evans built into his system amounts to a simple form of context-dependence.

People also have tactile pattern-recognition and this has received some attention within A.I. There are also forms of recognition not associated with any one sensory modality, such as the recognition by a doctor of a pattern of symptoms indicating a particular disease or the recognition by a meteorologist of a pattern in his data indicating the likelihood of a particular kind of weather.

PATTERN RECOGNITION AND LEARNING

Pattern recognition is an area where it seems particulary clear that human ability depends on learning from experience. A child learns to recognise the letters of the alphabet mainly by being shown numerous examples · and being told, for each, the correct classification. It is therefore usual to discuss pattern recognition together with learning.

In principle, a visual pattern-recogniser could operate by exhaustive classification. Suppose images are formed on a retina which is an array of light-sensitive elements. The input to a pattern-recognition system normally consists of signals from such an array — in one example the array is 32 elements wide and 48 high, making 1536 elements in all. Even for this grid (much coarser than a television picture), with each element producing a binary signal (black or white, no grey levels), the number of possible patterns is two raised to the power 1536, or approximately 10^{460}. A recogniser to work by exhaustive classification would have to allow, for each of this vast number of patterns, the possibility of associating a classification.

With such a large number of possible patterns, operation by exhaustive classification is not feasible. Even if the necessary storage were provided, the amount of experience required to fill it in by a learning process would be prohibitive.

Practical recognition systems operate by first processing the image to discover *features*, thereby obtaining a new representation with much-reduced information content. The *features* may have locations in the image area, or they may be generalised ones such as the answer to the question "Does the image contain a horizontal bar?".

Oliver Selfridge[1] has described a very general scheme for a learning system for pattern recognition. He termed it *Pandemonium* to emphasise the fact that it is best thought of as operating in a highly-parallel fashion. The elements within the *Pandemonium* are termed *demons*, and they are relatively-autonomous entities like Maxwell's Demon in Thermodynamics.

The lowest level of demons contains the *data* or *image* demons (Fig. 7.4), which could be the light-sensitive elements of a retina. Right at the top is the *decision demon* which decides the output of the whole system, namely an indication of a recognised pattern category. Below the decision demon are a number of *cognitive demons*, each corresponding to one of the pattern categories to be recognised.

The intention is that each *cognitive demon* should compute a measure of the degree of agreement of the incoming pattern imposed on the *data demons* with the pattern category represented by the *cognitive demon*. The better the agreement the stronger the signal sent to the *decision demon*, which then selects the strongest out of the signals reaching it.

It would be possible for the *cognitive demons* to receive their inputs directly from the *data demons*, but since there is some similarity between the requirements of the different *cognitive demons* it is more economical to insert stages of pre-processing which can be common to a number of cognitive demons. These are the *computational demons* and they correspond to the *feature* extractors of other schemes.

The *Pandemonium* is a learning device, and each cognitive demon keeps making adjustments in the way it combines the outputs of the computational demons to generate its own output to the decision

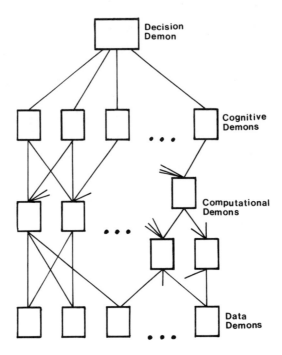

Fig. 7.4.   Selfridge's Pandemonium.

demon. This adjustment must depend on some feedback from the environment indicating the correctness or usefulness of the decisions. The feedback could be either in the form of a general indication of usefulness (degree of goal-achievement, to be used as the *objective function* for hill-climbing) or it could be an input from a "teacher", indicating retrospectively the correct classification. If the feedback is of this latter type, a *perceptron training algorithm* (see Chapter 8) can be used to control the learning process.

Selfridge assumes that all the cognitive demons compute weighted sums of the signals received from computational demons, so that the i-th cognitive demon computes its output D_i as:

$$D_i = \sum_j w_{ij} d_j$$

where the summation is over the computational demons and d_j is the output of the j-th computational demon.

The process of adjustment in the cognitive demon operates to adjust the weights w_{ij}. As indicated above, the means of adjustment must depend on the nature of the feedback to the whole system; if this is a scalar indication of degree of goal-achievement the adjustment must depend on true hill-climbing as described in Selfridge's paper.

Once the weights have been adjusted to approach an optimum set of values it is possible to compute, for any computational demon, a measure of its *worth* to the whole system. This depends on how much use is made of its output. A suitable measure of the *worth* of the *j*-th computational demon would be:

$$W_j = \sum_i |w_{ij}|$$

The computation of measures of *worth* allows changes in the available set of computational demons. Demons with low *worth* can be automatically eliminated and others generated to take their places. Thus the self-improvement of the *Pandemonium* comes to have a self-organizing character, and not just that of self-optimisation by the adjustment of parameters.

Selfridge suggests two ways in which new computational demons could be generated. Both of them are based on the idea that it is likely to be useful to generate demons having something in common with existing demons which have proved to have high *worth*. The two methods are *conjugation* and *mutated fission*.

Conjugation simply means that the outputs of two high-worth demons are combined, and if the outputs are of the logical or on-off type there are ten different ways in which they can be combined to form a new on-off signal. Selfridge suggests that an arbitrary choice be made from the ten.

In Fig. 7.4 one of the computational demons can be seen to be receiving inputs from two other demons; it is a demon which might have been instituted by *conjugation*. In order that the two contributing demons have appropriate measures of *worth* it is, of course, necessary that the demon receiving signals from the two makes contributions to their *worth* summations. The magnitude of these should presumably depend on the magnitude of its own *worth* summation. It can be seen that there could be feedback of contributions to *worth* measures through a long chain of elements in a network of this sort.

The present writer[2] has given attention to this *significance feedback* (and some variations on the theme) as a valuable feature of purposeful self-organizing networks. Although Selfridge postulates *conjugation* he does not discuss the need for this feedback over chains of elements. The general idea of preserving pathways which provide useful information is in broad agreement with the familiar behaviour of living systems. It is well known that muscles, in particular, become stronger with use and weaker with disuse. The same seems to be true of bones and there is evidence that sense-endings also develop with use.

The other proposal for the generation of new computational demons is *mutated fission*. The idea here is that new demons should be formed which are similar (but, of course, not identical) to those which have proved to have high *worth*. There is a difficulty in achieving the right kind of similarity in practice. It is necessary that demons be modified sufficiently that qualitatively-new types can arise. The representations of the demons must be such that mutations do not readily destroy the whole character (as changing one or a few binary digits in a machine-language computer program would usually do), and yet qualitatively-new forms of behaviour should be possible. The problem is similar to that of providing a means of introducing qualitatively-new terms in the static evaluation function in Samuel's checker-playing program. It is also related to Minsky's principle of *heuristic connection*.

In his original presentation of the *Pandemonium* principle, Oliver Selfridge discussed an application to the automatic reception of manually-transmitted Morse code. He found that the durations of dots and dashes and intervals were often not at all related in the standard way (a dash having three times the duration of a dot, the intervals within the code representation of a character being the same length as dots, and those between characters the same length as dashes).

The correct interpretation of the Morse symbols had to depend on examination of a length of the transmission in which it was embedded. This was achieved in a *Pandemonium* by letting the inputs to the data demons represent the length of message extending both ways from the symbol to be interpreted.

An application of the same general method to character recognition is described by Selfridge and Neisser[3]. The outputs of the computational demons are answers to questions such as that asked earlier as "Does the character contain a horizontal bar?". Other questions of the sort are "Does the character have more black area in its upper half than in its lower half?", "Is the character concave above?" and so on.

Character recognition with a low error rate was achieved. The method does not embody *mutated fission* in this practical application, however. In fact, the paper ends with the following acknowledgement of the shortcoming:

"The most important learning process is still untouched: No current program can generate test features of its own. The effectiveness of all of them is forever restricted by the ingenuity or arbitrariness of their programmers. We can barely guess how this restriction might be overcome. Until it is, 'artificial intelligence' will remain tainted with artifice."

FIXED-FOUNT RECOGNITION

The need to filter out features, by computational demons or equivalent systems under some other name, only arises if there is variation among the occurrences of the same character. In most commercial applications the characters are from a known fount and recognition is a matter of template-matching. The method needs to have some tolerance of discrepancies between characters and templates to allow for printing imperfections and dirt on the paper.

It is possible to compute a measure of the agreement between two images, of which one can be the input to be recognised and the other a stored template. Such a measure is sometimes termed a *spatial* (or two-dimensional) *cross-correlation*. A suitable measure is the fraction of the total area which is in agreement in the two images (i.e. black in both or white in both) when they are superimposed after adjustment to standard positions. If the images are the same this becomes unity.

A reading machine for fixed-fount operation can obtain the cross-correlation value for the input figure with each of the stored templates, and recognition is determined by the template giving the best agreement. If no template gives good agreement, or at least an agreement standing out above the others, the indication can be "don't know".

The fount used for the reference numbers on gas and electricity bills has been carefully designed to have a low spatial cross-correlation between the characters of the fount.

DISTRIBUTED FEATURES

A system to recognise multi-fount and hand-blocked characters has been described by John Parks[4] of the National Physical Laboratory. His system is aimed at commercial applications, where there is a continuing need to transfer data from documents into digital machines.

The system begins with a representation of the character in a 32 × 48 array of small square elements of area (sometimes termed *pixels*). This is scanned to identify line segments orientated in different ways. The scanning is done electronically, but is exactly as though a frame with a 7 × 7 array of photocells was placed over every sub-area of the image containing 7 × 7 pixels.

The frame is, in effect, made to scan the image by moving right across it horizontally, a pixel (not a frame-width) at a time, and then dropping down one pixel to scan across again and so on. In every position the photocell output is examined and certain comparisons are made between groups of photocells.

Fig. 7.5 shows one of the comparisons which would be made between sub-groups of photocells; the average output of those marked with a

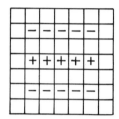

Fig. 7.5. Connections to sampling points in grid as used to scan for horizontal line segments.

plus sign would be compared with the average of those marked with a minus. If the picture was darker under the *plus* cells there is evidence of a roughly-horizontal line segment in this area. The rows of cells are of length five although they could have been of length seven; it was necessary to avoid too strong discrimination of direction.

A similar comparison of photocells in vertical rows detected roughly-vertical segments. Comparison of cells in diagonal lines, as shown for one of the two possibilities in Fig. 7.6 , detected sloping segments.

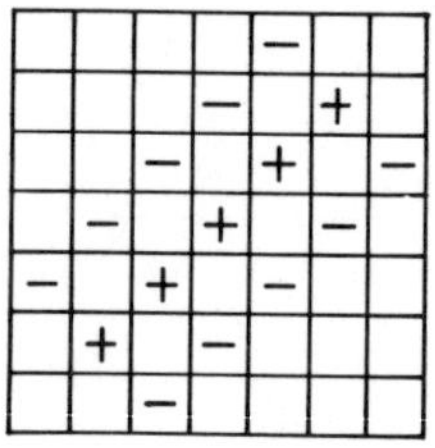

Fig. 7.6. Connections to sampling points in grid as used to scan for line segments sloping up-wards to the right.

In this way, the array of pixels, each with a brightness indication, was turned into an array of cells of which some carried an indication of the detection of a line segment in some direction. (These cells could store two or even three directions in a cell, in case there was evidence of a line segment but two or three directions were indicated fairly equally.)

The new array was again scanned by a 7×7 grid which, if certain conditions were met, would indicate detection of a *morphological feature* of the character. A *morphological feature* could be the *termination* of a line (allowed for in 8 orientations), or a *direction-change* (allowed for as acute, right-angled and obtuse, each with 8 orientations), or a *junction* or a *crossover*. Allowing for varieties and orientations, there are 54 different morphological features in all.

Fig. 7.7 represents the necessary conditions among the elements under the grid during the second scan, in order to indicate the termination of a line coming horizontally from the left.

The representation of the character is thus reduced to a listing of morphological features along with an approximate indication of their positions in the character area. A fairly simple computer program, devised on the basis of a great deal of statistical data from sloppily-made characters, can go from the list of features to a pretty reliable identification of the character.

The initial scanning of the image by the grid of virtual photocells, and the detection of line segments, corresponds remarkably closely to what has been found to be an early stage in the processing of images in the visual cortex of the mammalian brain. This is discussed in Chapter 12.

	$\bar{V}$	$\bar{V}$	$\bar{V}$	$\bar{D}$	$\bar{D}$	
	$\bar{V}$	$\bar{V}$	$\bar{V}$	$\bar{D}$	$\bar{D}$	
	H				$\bar{H}$	$\bar{H}$
H	H	H	H		$\bar{H}$	$\bar{H}$
	H				$\bar{H}$	$\bar{H}$
	$\bar{V}$	$\bar{V}$	$\bar{V}$	$\bar{d}$	$\bar{d}$	
	$\bar{V}$	$\bar{V}$	$\bar{V}$	$\bar{d}$	$\bar{d}$	

Fig. 7.7.　Grid connections used in the second-stage scan to detect the termination of a horizontal line coming from the left. The requirement for a response is that cells marked with an "H" must occupy a position at which a horizontal line segment was detected in the first scan, and similarly (if there were any) for "V" (vertical segment), "D" (segment sloping up to the right) and "d" (segment sloping the other way). Where a letter appears with a bar the cell is allowed to correspond to anything except what the letter represents. This seemingly-arbitrary criterion of detection of the morphological feature is the result of much experimentation; it must be neither too rigid nor too loose.

AUDITORY PERCEPTION

A spoken word or sentence,or any other sound-pattern, can be turned into a two-dimensional picture without loss of the essential information. The picture is termed a sound-spectrogram and normally has time as the horizontal axis and frequency (say from 50 to 3000 or 4000 Hertz) as the vertical axis. Sound energy of a particular frequency at a particular time is represented by darkening of the appropriate point on the spectrogram.

Sound spectrograms produced in real time have been used to allow deaf people to "hear" speech by watching a display screen, and it is possible for a deaf person to carry on a conversation with this aid.

Since the sound spectrogram is possible, recognition methods for spoken words can be very like those for printed characters and other visual patterns. The *features* derived from the spectrogram are likely to be rather simpler than, for example, the *morphological features* of Parks's scheme. For the spectrogram, the features are likely to be simply the appearance of a significant amount of energy in a particular frequency-time cell. A complication is that words are"elastic" in the time dimension, having much the same significance when spoken quickly or slowly or with syllables compressed and expanded. In the frequency dimension the same elasticity does not apply; fairly definite *formant frequencies* are characteristic of vowel sounds.

As mentioned earlier, artificial speech recognition can be achieved provided the vocabulary of possible words is small, and it can be useful with this restriction. The principle of the *Perceptron* (see next chapter) can be applied in a word-recognition system to let it be trained to the voice of a particular speaker.

What the human auditory system can achieve is truly remarkable; conversations can be carried on under cocktail-party conditions or over telephone links with severe distortion and interference. The human perception of speech is not just a matter of word or phoneme-recognition, however — there is a complex interaction of processes at many levels. This will be discussed in the next chapter under the heading of *Knowledge Engineering*.

CLUSTER ANALYSIS

In the discussion so far it has been assumed that the categories of pattern to be recognised were known in advance. A versatile system to learn recognition might reasonably be expected to discover the categories for itself. Some schemes for character recognition have been able to "learn without a teacher". That is to say, they could be presented with a great many samples of letters and would decide for themselves that there were 26 patterns in what was presented (or 52 if upper and lower case were included).

Any scheme of this kind, operating with no feedback of the usefulness of the classification it produces, must somehow have been pushed a little in the direction of the required result. Without some feedback of utility, letters could equally well be classified as fat ones and thin ones, or ones with enclosed areas and ones without.

Some types of pattern recognition depend on metrical information, and inputs can be represented by points in some phase space. For example, if the heights and weights of people are plotted as in Fig. 7.8, it would appear from this sample that the individuals come from two populations, and the corresponding points are separated by the broken line. Having drawn this line it is possible to recognise new individuals as being members of one or other of the classes once their heights and weights are known.

There is an extensive literature on ways of determining discriminating lines like that in Fig. 7.8 (see Sebestyen[5]). In three dimensions a

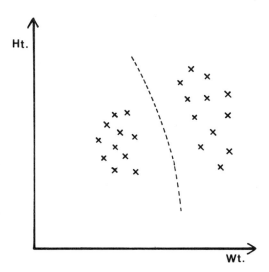

Fig. 7.8. A *scatter diagram* in which each point represents an individual, plotted in a position determined by weight and height. The broken line separates two *clusters* of individuals.

discriminating surface would be found, and in higher dimensionality a hyper-surface. Sometimes the discriminating line or surface is derived on the basis of a known classification. Where the classification is deduced from the data itslf, as in the situation represented in Fig. 7.8, the operation is an example of *Cluster Analysis*.

REFERENCES

1. O.G. Selfridge, "Pandemonium: a paradigm for learning" *Mechanisation of Thought Processes* (HMSO, London, 1959) pp. 511-531.

2. A.M. Andrew, "Significance feedback and redundancy reduction in self-organizing networks" In: *Advances in Cybernetics and Systems Science* 1, F. Pichler and R. Trappl (Ed) (*Transcripta*, London, 1973) pp. 244-252.

3. O.G. Selfridge and U. Neisser, "Pattern recognition by machine" In: *Computers and Thought* E.A. Feigenbaum and J. Feldman (Ed) (McGraw-Hill, New York, 1963) pp. 237-250.

4. J.R. Parks, "A multi-level system of analysis for mixedfont and hand-blocked printed characters recognition" in: *Automatic Interpretation and Classification of Images* A. Grasselli (Ed) (Academic Press, New York, 1969) Ch. 15, 295-322.

5. G.S. Sebestyen, *Decision-Making Processes in Pattern Recognition* (Macmillan, New York, 1972).

Chapter 8

SCENE ANALYSIS

Many important kinds of perception cannot be represented as the recognition of patterns from a finite set of possibilities. Even where they can, difficulties can stem, as previously mentioned, from the impossibility of separating the images of discrete objects. Particularly with increasing interest in Robotics there has been particular attention to *Scene Analysis* in recent years.

Although it still leaves many important problems unresolved, what was seen as something of a breakthrough was the development of methods for the interpretation of line drawings of polyhedral objects and groups of such objects. Fig. 8.1 is an example of the kind of drawing which can be analysed. (See discussion by Minsky and Papert[1]).

The interpretation of line drawings is probably more relevant to the wider problem of scene analysis than might at first appear. An early stage in the analysis of visual scenes is probably the identification of boundaries. Computer programs usually start in this way, and the work of Hubel and Wiesel (see Chapter 12) shows that something similar happens in the mammalian visual cortex.

Furthermore, Hubel and Wiesel have shown that boundaries and line segments are both detected at the same stage of processing in the brain. It is therefore likely that the two are taken into account in similar ways in later processing. Certainly, line drawings are accepted by people with remarkable readiness as representations of solid objects, consistent with the suggestion that images of solid objects are processed to become

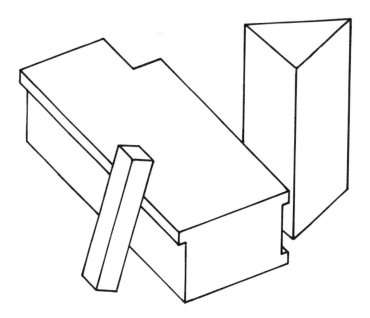

Fig. 8.1. Line drawing of a group of polyhedral solids.

equivalent to line drawings.

Needless to say, the world is not filled with polyhedra and line drawings of real-world objects are not composed exclusively of straight lines. Straight-line drawings provide a starting-point and work is in progress to develop techniques for pictures with curves.

The analysis of a picture like Fig. 8.1 depends on *labelling* the lines in different ways according to what they represent in the picture. A line must represent one of the following:

(a) A concave edge.

(b) A convex edge, both of the adjacent faces being visible.

(c) A convex edge with only one adjacent face visible — the lines which form the outline of the object are in this group.

It is assumed that the objects in the picture are such that no more than three planes meet at any point (so square pyramids are excluded). It is also assumed that the point of view is such that any small change of the viewer's position does not alter the set of vertices and line-junctions seen.

The simplest way a computer program can start to interpret a line picture like Fig. 8.1 is by labelling all the lines to indicate whether they belong to (a), (b) or (c). The system of labelling is termed Huffman-Clowes labelling, after the two workers who invented it independently. The usual convention is that lines of type (a) are marked with a minus sign ($-$) and lines of type (b) with plus ($+$). Lines of type (c) are a little more complicated to deal with, since it is desirable that the labelling indicates on which side there is the visible face of the solid. The convention is to mark such lines with an arrowhead, with the visible face to the right of the arrow.

It is easily seen that there are restrictions on the combinations of types of line which can meet at a junction. These are sufficiently strong that there is only one way of labelling the lines in a given picture (if it is a picture of a genuine possible object subject to the above two assumptions).

The outer edge of the picture can only be made up of lines of type (c), and clearly the arrowheads must follow each other round in a clockwise direction.

The constraints which allow the labelling of all the lines arise from the fact that there are only four possible types of corner of a polyhedral solid (subject to the assumptions). The four are illustrated in Fig. 8.2, and the possible views of them, with labelling of the adjacent lines, are shown in Fig. 8.3. It is also possible to have three kinds of T-junction, as represented in Fig. 8.4.

Fig. 8.5 shows a picture of the kind which can be analysed, with Huffman-Clowes labelling. It is somewhat simpler than Fig. 8.1. (Fig. 8.1 is well within the capabilities of existing programs, however.) Once the labelling has been carried out it is possible to list the distinct objects in the picture and to list their faces. To do this it is also necessary to look for sets of lines which are in exact alignment, like the two pairs of vertical ones which are obviously the edges of a triangular prism in Fig. 8.5, and to associate these sets as a single line.

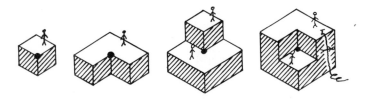

Fig. 8.2.   The four possible types of corner in polyhedral solids (after Raphael[2]). Horizontal upper surfaces are indicated by standing figures; another figure is abseiling down a vertical face.

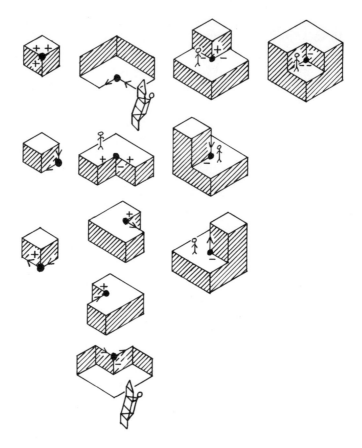

Fig. 8.3. All the ways the four types of corner can be seen as Y-junctions or bends, with labelling of adjacent lines (after Raphael[2]). Horizontal lower surfaces are indicated by figures hanging from étriers.

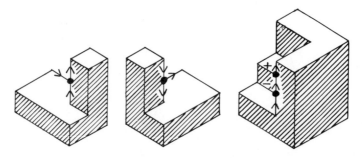

Fig. 8.4. The four possible types of T-junction, with labelling of adjacent lines (after Raphael[2]).

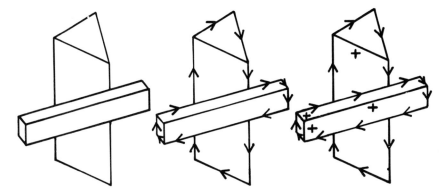

Fig. 8.5.   Line drawing with no labelling, with labelling of lines in boundary, and with full labelling.

KNOWLEDGE ENGINEERING

The above method achieves analysis of complex scenes of a particular type, but human scene-analysis is a much more complicated matter. It utilises information from many sources and of many types.

In the real three-dimensional world we have, at least for near objects, the benefit of stereoscopic depth-perception, using the two eyes as a range-finder. This is of course not available when interpreting a two-dimensional picture of a scene, and from the effectiveness with which people do this it is clear that the analysis process has many more "tricks up its sleeve".

The analysis process certainly uses information conveyed by shadows cast by the objects, and by differences in the brightness of illumination of the faces of the objects. It is for this reason that some judicious shading of surfaces in figures like Figs. 8.2 to 8.4 can greatly aid their interpretation.

The inclusion of pin-men in these figures illustrates a further point, namely that the analysis favours interpretations which are consistent with what is known about gravity and other physical constraints. In conformity with this, interpretations according to which objects are supported are preferred to ones which require them to be floating in space.

Also, something is usually known about the types of object likely to be encountered and probable spatial relationships. The general idea has been indicated by the remark: "If we have recognised a leg we know where to look for a foot". Actually, as the late Max Clowes pointed out, this way of putting it makes the situation seem simpler than it is. A better indication is given by saying: "If we have tentatively identified a leg and a foot in a particular relationship, and suitably positioned with respect to other fully or tentatively-recognised objects, then with a high level of confidence we can identify the combination as a nether limb".

Much of A.I. is concerned with the interactions of knowledge acquired in many different ways and having many different complexions. The term *Knowledge Engineering* has been used to refer to A.I. studies, emphasising this aspect.

Max Clowes believed that the problems of *Knowledge Engineering* could be studied most profitably in the context of visual perception. Other workers have concentrated on speech recognition, which similarly involves many different kinds of knowledge.

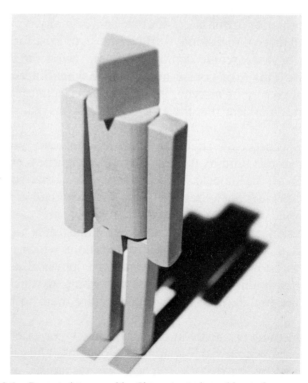

Fig. 8.6.   Puppet picture used by Clowes to study problems of scene analysis.

Clowes set himself the task of writing computer programs which would accept, as input, pictures of a small pin-jointed puppet figure, like Fig. 8.6. The puppet could be placed in different positions, and the idea was to incorporate in the program information on the physical constraints of the puppet. The program was to use this information in interpreting the input picture (with regard to shadows and support of the puppet) to generate a description of the puppet's position.

Speech recognition, in a similar though perhaps even more complicated way, requires the combination of a great many kinds of knowledge. Early work on speech recognition tended to assume a progression from the recognition of phonemes to that of words and then, using the rules of syntax, to sentences and finally to meaning.

In fact, the process is much more complex than this linear progression. The recognition of phonemes is influenced by tentative recognition of words and meanings; the recognition of words is influenced by syntactic and semantic considerations. As will be seen in the next chapter, the extraction of meaning depends on the continuous interplay of semantic and syntactic analysis.

Speech analysis is also influenced by clues coming from the speaker's modulation of his voice, both in pitch and volume. If the speaker is visible, information relevant to recognition comes from the facial expression and gestures. The process must also adapt to the speaker's accent and other characteristics and to the conditions of reverberation. One project on speech recognition used an array of minicomputers to analyse in parallel the different relevant aspects of the speech, the outputs finally being combined in a central machine, termed the *Recognition Overlord*.

SYNTAX AND PATTERN RECOGNITION

Any process of recognition requires some representation of the pattern categories to be recognised. Where template-matching is acceptable the representations are in the templates. In most applications there is some variation between samples of the same pattern category and the requirements of the recognition task are not easy to formulate.

It is necessary to have a form of representation of the categories which indicates just what is invariant from one sample to another in the same category. Even in the relatively simple task of recognising hand-blocked characters it is not easy to say what is invariant from one sample, say of the letter A, to another. The classification is unchanged by a moderate amount of the kind of distortion produced by writing the character on a rubber sheet and pulling it about. However, it is also unaffected by the addition of some extra lines, as in Fig. 8.7, or by small breaks in some lines.

Fig. 8.7.   Poorly-formed examples of letter "A" having more lines than in standard form.

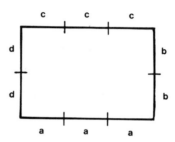

Fig. 8.8.   Rectangle to be represented syntactically.

Ideally, the pattern category should be represented in a way which is general enough to cover all the permitted variations but distinguishes the category from others. A natural-language description (say, of a capital A as consisting of two lines meeting at the top but apart at the foot, with a cross-bar about half way up) often seems to meet the requirement better than other forms of representation.

There is consequently interest in the use of linguistic methods in visual pattern-recognition. Formal methods for dealing with syntax are introduced in Appendix 3 of Chapter 13, where sets of *productions* or *rewrite rules* are given which define a *sentence* and a *simple arithmetic expression*.

The general idea behind the syntactic representation of pictures is that the patterns should be represented by sets of *production rules*. This requires that the patterns be built up by combining smaller fragments, and some form of primitive constituent must be recognised. The primitive constituents can, for example, be straight line segments of fixed length.

Suppose the symbols *a*, *b*, *c* and *d* are used to denote straight-line segments of standard length, such that a segment *a* is drawn from left to right, a *b* goes vertically upward, a *c* is from right to left and a *d* is vertically downward. Then the rectangle of Fig. 8.8, starting from its lower left-hand corner and going round it counter-clockwise, could be represented by *aaabbcccdd*. This uses the convention that the succession of symbols corresponds to end-to-end concatenation of the line segments.

A general expression for a non-tilted rectangle would be:

$$a^n b^m c^n d^m$$

where *n* and *m* are positive integers

Although the Backus-Naur Form, as introduced in Appendix 3 of Chapter 13, allows indefinite repetition, it does not provide the means of ensuring the *a* is repeated the same number of times as *c*, and *b* the same as *d*. However, other varieties of formal syntax can be used in visual pattern-recognition (see review by Fu[3]).

PERCEPTRONS

The term *perceptron* was coined by Frank Rosenblatt to refer to a class of pattern-recognition systems able to learn from experience. He introduced the idea in the nineteen-fifties, and for a time it aroused great interest (and also considerable resentment from workers following other lines who felt Rosenblatt had oversold the idea and attracted an undue share of research funding).

The *perceptron* belongs to the older generation of pattern-recognition systems, in that it assumes the pattern to be recognised can be seen in isolation. This shortcoming, and others, are discussed by Minsky and Papert[1] in their book which was influential in bringing about the shift in emphasis in pattern-recognition research.

A perceptron is made up of threshold elements intended to model nerve cells (neurons) as first suggested by McCulloch and Pitts[4]. Some of the parameters of some of the model neurons are adjusted in the course of learning. Despite the shortcomings, the principle is of interest because the *perceptron training algorithm*, used in making the adjustments, can form a part of a more comprehensive learning system. Also, at the time it was put forward, the idea crystalised something definite out of a mass of rather diffuse speculation about self-adjusting networks of neuron-like elements. (Such crystalisation has its drawbacks — it must not be assumed that everything of value in earlier work is subsumed in the perceptron.)

The device is usually described as a scheme for visual pattern-recognition, but it can also be used in other modalities. In conjuction with frequency analysis and time delays (equivalent to drawing the spectrogram), it can be used for word recognition, for example.

A perceptron contains units of three kinds, as shown in Fig. 8.9. The *sensory units* or *s-units* could be the light-sensitive elements of a retina; they correspond to the data or image demons of Selfridge's *Pandemonium*. It is generally assumed the s-units are on-off devices but this need not be so.

The next layer of units contains *association units* or *a-units*, which correspond roughly to the computational demons of a *Pandemonium*. In the standard perceptron their connections from s-units are formed randomly when the system is first set up, so the outputs are a haphazard set of "properties" of the image. A variant of the perceptron has been described by Roberts[5], and this computes an indication of *worth* for each *a-unit*, just as in the *Pandemonium*. Any *a-unit* proving to have low *worth* after some time of operation has its input connections disbanded and new set chosen randomly (or pseudo-randomly — see Appendix 2 of Chapter 1).

The outputs of the *a-units* go to a set of *response units* or *r-units*, corresponding to the cognitive demons of a *Pandemonium*. It is usual to consider only one *r-unit* in discussions of the principle of operation, the

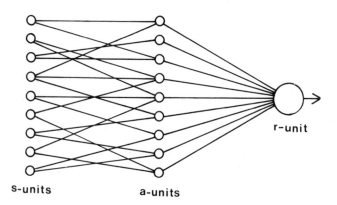

Fig. 8.9.   Simple Perceptron.

argument being that if one category can be recognised others can be treated similarly. It is assumed that each r-unit gives a "yes" or "no" answer and there is no need for anything corresponding to a decision demon to choose among them.

In their early paper, McCulloch and Pitts discussed the kind of computation that could go on in a nervous system. They introduced the idea of a "model neuron" whose properties correspond roughly to those of real living neurons. A "model neuron" is a threshold element; it has a number of input connections, each either active or not active at any one time. (This corresponds to the all-or-none law of nervous conduction.) Some of the inputs to the model neuron have an excitatory effect, others an inhibitory one. Each model neuron has a certain *threshold* value, and if the number of excitatory inputs active at the same time exceeds the threshold, and no inhibitory ones are active at the same time, the neuron "fires" to give an output signal.

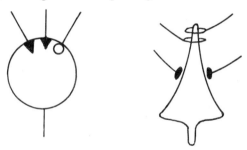

Fig. 8.10.   Representations of model neurons.

Fig. 8.10 shows two representations of model neurons. Sometimes they are drawn to correspond to the shape of some real neurons, and sometimes a plain circle is used. In either case an input ending in a black dot or triangle is excitatory and one ending in a little circle is inhibitory. Every neuron has one outgoing pathway, corresponding to the *axon* of a real neuron. A number may be written inside the neuron to show the threshold. Fig. 8.11 shows model neurons computing the logical functions AND, OR and NOT.

For the purpose of modelling aspects of nervous-system activity in artificial systems a slight departure is often made from the McCulloch-Pitts model. It requires a simple count of the excitatory inputs active. There is evidence that one of the mechanisms of learning in the nervous system is modification of the *synapses* or points at which an axon of one

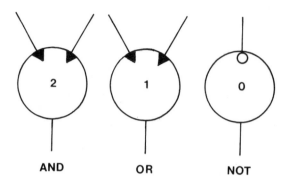

Fig. 8.11. Model neurons computing logical functions.

neuron can influence another one. This can be modelled by letting a *weight* value be associated with each synapse. Then, instead of simply counting the active excitatory synapses, their *weights* are summed.

Inhibitory synapses can be assumed to have negative weights and can then be included in the summation. This is contrary to the original proposal of McCulloch and Pitts, who gave inhibitory synapses an absolute power of veto, but it is convenient to let all synapses be treated uniformly. Under the new assumptions, the condition for a model neuron to "fire" and give an output is:

$$\sum_i x_i w_i \geq t$$

where the summation is over all the inputs to the neuron, w_i is the *weight* of the i-th synapse, t is the threshold, and x_i takes value 1 or 0 depending on whether or not the i-th input is active.

Both the *a-units* and the *r-units* of a perceptron are model neurons of this revised kind. Some of the connections from *s-units* to *a-units* are excitatory and some inhibitory. The weights of the synapses to the *r-units* are altered by a learning process termed a *perceptron training algorithm*.

For the *training algorithm* to work it is necessary that, in the training period, each output or "guess" of the perceptron is followed by an indication from a "teacher" as to whether or not it was correct. Then the usual form of the training algorithm operates as follows.

If the response of the r-unit is correct (i.e. it fires and the pattern belongs to the category to be recognised, or it does not fire and the pattern does not belong), no change is made in the weights. If it fails to fire for a pattern which does belong, the weights of synapses which were active are increased by an amount c. On the other hand, if it fires for a pattern which does not belong, the weights of synapses which were active are reduced by c.

The capabilities of perceptrons have been investigated mathematically and a theorem termed the *Convergence Theorem* is a candidate for being the "world's most-proved theorem" on account of the many different proofs advanced for it. Two of the most succinct have been selected by Nilsson[6]. Roughly speaking, the Convergence Theorem states that, if there is a set of weight values which will allow a particular discrimination, the training algorithm will eventually reach either it or an equivalent set, so that the discrimination is achieved.

To state the theorem rigorously it is necessary to refer to conditions to be satisfied by the sequence of input patterns. This must contain samples from a finite set of possibilities, of which some are and some are not, members of the category to be recognised. The method of generation of the sequence must be such that there is no limit to the number of presentations of any pattern in the set; each would appear infinitely often in an infinitely long sequence.

The Convergence Theorem has sometimes been presented as the ultimate vindication of the perceptron principle, but in fact it leaves several important questions unanswered. In the first place it has nothing to say about which discriminations *can* be performed — this is completely by-passed in the statement of the theorem. Minsky and Papert have shown that there are severe restrictions on the discriminations that can be performed by a *simple perceptron*. (What has been described here is a *simple perceptron*. Rosenblatt left his definition sufficiently vague that it is not easy to say exactly which schemes are and are not to be classed as perceptrons.) The suggestions made in early work on perceptrons, that such systems could learn by experience the abstract principles of invariance of patterns under dilatation, translation and rotation, are not now taken seriously.

Minsky and Papert also point out that the Convergence Theorem only guarantees ultimate convergence; it gives no indication of the number of presentations needed to reach it, nor of whether the convergent state requires the adjustment of weight values to an impossible degree of precision.

Nevertheless, the perceptron principle is a useful weapon in the programmer's armoury whenever classifiers are to be trained in the "with a teacher" situation. A system to recognise spoken words from a small vocabulary is in this situation when given sample inputs to allow adjustment to the characteristics of a particular speaker.

REFERENCES

1. M. Minsky and S. Papert, *Perceptrons* (MIT Press, Cambridge, Mass., 1969).
2. B. Raphael, *The Thinking Computer: Mind Inside Matter* (Freeman, San Francisco, 1976).
3. K.S. Fu, "Syntactic (linguistic) pattern recognition" *Digital Pattern Recognition* K.S. Fu (Ed) (Springer, Berlin, 1976) Ch. 4, pp. 95-134.
4. W.S. McCulloch and W. Pitts, "A logical calculus of the ideas immanent in nervous activity" *Bull. Math. Biophysics* **5**, 115-137 (1943).
5. L.G. Roberts, "Pattern recognition with an adaptive network" *IRE International Convention Record*, part 2, 66-70 (1960).
6. N.J. Nilsson, *Learning Machines* (McGraw-Hill, New York, 1965) Ch. 5, pp. 79-94.

Chapter 9

USING NATURAL LANGUAGE

For a variety of reasons, there is interest in computer programs to use natural language in some way. As has been mentioned, speech is a natural form of communication for people, and computer users would like to able to talk to their machines. Natural language input can be presented either as speech or in the form of text inserted at a keyboard.

The high-level programming languages in common use contain many natural-language words; the *ALGOL* languages use BEGIN, END, FOR, WHILE, IF, THEN, ELSE and some others, and some of these are used also in *FORTRAN* and *BASIC*. Programming languages embodying these words (used in essentially their everyday sense) makes the task of programming enormously simpler than it is in the *machine language* or even in an *assembly language* (which makes some concessions to human convenience). However, these high-level languages are still very different from ordinary natural-language communication, and have to be learned.

Apart from programming computers, people want to interact with them when the programs are running, to command them and question them. Again, the more freely natural language can be used, the happier the users are likely to be (though some reservations will appear in the following).

It is also convenient if the messages from the machine to the user can be in natural language, particularly if they are of some complexity. This is not so difficult to arrange as is the acceptance by the machine of natural-language input.

The term *natural language* tends to be used with the assumption that what is meant is English. Because much of the poineering work of A.I. has been done in U.S.A. it is very much in an English-speaking environment, and it is sometimes forgotten that other languages are "natural" in other parts of the world. There was once even a research proposal put forward for a scheme to translate *natural language* into German!

A type of program which must communicate with its users in complex ways is an *expert system* as discussed in the next chapter. Such programs are applied to tasks such as medical diagnosis, and it is important that they are able to justify any conclusion they reach. A user of some of these systems can give the command "explain" and the system gives, in a fairly good approximation to conversational English, an account of the chain of steps by which it reached its conclusion.

This sort of response can greatly aid man-machine interaction. It has been argued that in a recent failure in a nuclear power plant, the computer systems had been designed on the assumption that the warning itself, in a sufficiently loud and clear form, was what mattered. The operator did not have the facility for requesting an explanation, which would have been helpful in deciding on emergency action. He was, instead, thrown into confusion by flashing lights and hooters.

Apart from these matters of user interaction there is a deeper reason for interest in natural language in A.I. Humans make use of language in their internal reasoning as well as in communicating outside themselves. If the intelligence of computers is to simulate human thinking it should also use natural language internally.

This last point raises rather deep questions about the nature of thought, and the extent to which it is linguistic. In some contexts the verbal part is the "tip of the iceberg" but in others it is more fundamental.

Another area in which the use of machines to process natural language has been considered is that of *Mechanical Translation* between natural languages. It is hardly necessary to comment on the potential usefulness of this, if it could be achieved. Many of the difficulties of dealing with natural language in programs became apparent in the course of studies aimed at producing programs for Mechanical Translation.

SYNTAX

The rules by which sentences are formed in a language seem fairly definite and at first sight it would appear to be possible to break down the sentences of natural-language input in essentially the way it is done in *parsing* or *analysis* as taught in school. If it is possible to recognise words as belonging to the "parts of speech" categories of *noun*, *adjective*, *verb*, etc., it would seem to be a small step to analyse sentences into *subject* and *predicate*, and predicate into *verb* and *object*, and so on. Having analysed a sentence according to its syntax it should be possible to extract its meaning.

Unfortunately, things are not so simple. The process of *analysis* as required in the classroom depends much more on an understanding of the *semantics* or meaning of the sentence than was realised before attempts were made to automate it. It is not difficult to illustrate, by means of specially-chosen sentences, that the interpretation of natural language depends heavily on knowledge of the subject matter.

One simple way in which interpretation depends on subject-matter is in resolving the meaning of ambiguous words. The linguist Bar-Hillel used the following pair of sentences (now often called "Bar-Hillel's paradox") to illustrate this:

> The pen is in the box.
> The box is in the pen.

The word *pen* in the first sentence suggests a pen for writing, whereas in the second a *pen* of a quite different kind is suggested, namely an enclosure for animals. There is nothing in the syntax to suggest this difference of meaning, which would be important in translating the sentences into a language in which there was no one word to cover the two meanings of "pen".

Sometimes the influence of the semantics on the interpretation is more subtle, as in the following pair of sentences quoted by Winograd[1]:

"The city fathers refused to give the women a permit to demonstrate, because they feared violence."

"The city fathers refused to give the women a permit to demonstrate, because they favoured revolution."

In the first of these, the pronoun *they* is assumed to refer to the city fathers, who are more likely to worry about violence than is a group of militant women. In the second sentence the pronoun almost certainly refers to the women since it is unthinkable that city fathers would favour revolution. In translating these sentences into a language in which the pronoun equivalent to *they* had masculine and feminine forms, it would be necessary to make a different choice for the two sentences.

Sometimes the meanings suggested by context are in some conflict, as in the following:

"The old man's glasses were filled with sherry."

Most people reading this first interpret *glasses* as referring to spectacles (the word *old* encourages this) and then backtrack to alter the interpretation when the later part is read.

The ambiguities to be resolved by semantic considerations are not confined to ambiguous words and pronoun references. It can happen that the structure of a sentence can only be decided by reference to semantics. A somewhat artificial example is the sentence:

Time flies.

In one interpretation this is a statement about the passage of time, but it could alternatively be a command to obtain data with the help of a stopwatch about movements of insects.

A more convincing example, again due to Winograd, is the pair of sentences:

"He hit the car with the rock."
"He hit the car with the dented fender."

The most natural interpretation of the first sentence makes the prepositional phrase an adverbial one associated with the verb *hit*. In the second sentence it most likely refers to the noun *car* and plays the part of an adjective. There is nothing in the form of the two sentences to indicate this difference in syntax.

Phrases beginning with the word *with* are often used where, as above, the sentence structure gives little indication of their reference. Even the following sentence, due to Schank[2] can be interpreted quite readily by a person, but clearly only by use of semantics:

"I hit the boy with the girl with long hair with a hammer with vengeance."

The matter of pronoun reference was raised earlier. Usually a pronoun such as *it* refers to a noun fairly near it in the text. Proximity is not an infallible guide, however. This is illustrated in one discussion by quoting a story in which Mary had bought a kite for John. She mentions this to Joan, who says "No, John already has a kite, and he would make you take it back".

There is no doubt in the minds of readers that the *it* in Joan's comment refers to the kite which Mary bought, but this certainly could not have been deduced from proximity considerations alone.

It is clear that in any useful analysis of natural-language text, analysis of the syntax and of the semantics must go hand-in-hand. This is in fact a subdivision of the problem of *knowledge engineering* involved in speech recognition.

The need to utilise semantic information has two important consequences. The first is that work on *Mechanical Translation* has virtually been abandoned, even though a great deal of effort was expended on it in the nineteen-fifties. A machine to do high-quality translation would need to embody much of the experience and view of the world of a human being, to a degree which is well beyond present possibilities.

The second consequence is that an artificial system to utilise natural language, in a way that remotely resembles the freedom of the human use of it, must restrict discussion to a particular *universe of discourse*. In one of the most successful projects this has been a piece of three-dimensional space containing a box and some coloured cubes and pyramids.

The space and its contents had no physical embodiment outside the computer memory, but this did not prevent them being viewed on a colour television screen. Before discussing this famous work of Winograd[1], some further comments will be made on the ambiguity of language.

LANGUAGE AMBIGUITY

The ambiguities mentioned up to now have been mainly ones which would hamper language translation. There are also ambiguities of *meaning* which are important if the computer program has to respond to the content of natural-language messages. These ambiguities would not necessarily hamper a translation process as they can be carried over in the translation.

Because of the various ambiguities, unrestricted natural language is not an ideal means of communication with computers. (Nor is it for interpersonal communication under all circumstances. Mathematics is conveyed by special symbolisms, and high-level programming languages can help one person to explain an algorithmic procedure to another without necessarily involving a computer. Such things as military drill and refereeing of games are best done in a pre-arranged subset of the language.)

It has been suggested by Hill[3] that, rather than trying to arrange to program computers in ordinary English, a more useful goal might be to let our way of communicating with people embody characteristics of programming languages.

The simple ambiguity of words does not always disappear so conveniently as it seems to in Bar Hillel's paradox. It is difficult to be *quite* certain of the meaning of:

"You'd hardly know little Johnny now. He's grown another foot."

Natural language is often ambiguous because it does not include anything corresponding to the brackets used in mathematics and in high-level programming languages to indicate priorities of operators. The phrase:

Old men and women

is ambiguous in that no one can be sure whether it is meant to include women who are not old. If brackets were allowed, young women would be included in:

(Old men) and women

but not in

Old (men and women)

There can be ambiguity in the reference of adverbs like *again,* as in the following piece of dialogue:

"I feel like going to bed with Bridgitte Bardot again tonight."
"Again?"
"Yes, I have felt like it before."

The meaning attached to words may be strongly context-dependent. An example quoted by Hill contrasts the use of the word *usually* in the following:

"Do you usually enjoy your holidays?"
"Do you usually enjoy good health?"

As Hill points out, an insurance company would not be pleased with a client who answered "yes" to the second question, interpreting *usually* as in the first, so that his reply meant "During the rare periods when I am in good health, I do usually enjoy it."

Conditional statements of the "If .... then ...." form are often used in such a way that the pre-condition is not so precise as is necessary in the programming context. If I say to a friend "If I had not come to this conference I would have gone to the one in London", the friend understands that my statement is only true if a number of other circumstances remain unchanged. It is for example understood though not stated that I would not have gone to the London conference if my reason for missing the present one was a nasty accident which left me in no fit state to attend any conference. A similar set of unspoken assumptions is associated with most statements about causality.

Lawyers try to overcome the inherent ambiguities of natural language by expressing laws and documents in an extremely cumbersome version of it. Despite their efforts ambiguities are by no means uncommon and judgements have to be given according to what seems to have been the intention of a law rather than on what it clearly states.

These somewhat derogatory remarks about natural language should not be allowed to obscure its power and generality. It has been described as our *Ultimate Metalanguage*[4] in which the special terms and symbols of even formal mathematical and programming languages are ultimately defined.

Although there are great difficulties in enabling programs to respond to unrestricted natural language, considerable success has been achieved within very restricted contexts and with restrictions on permitted syntactic forms.

An early question-answering program[5] was able to answer questions about baseball, on the basis of stored data on all the games in the American League for one year. For each game there was a record of the month, day, place, teams and score.

The program is able to answer questions in a range of formats, from simple ones like:

"Who did the Red Sox lose to on July 5?"
"Where did the Red Sox play on July 7?"

to complex ones like:

"Did every team play at least once in each park in each month?"

A variety of types of question beginning with "How many" could be answered. Not surprisingly, the system is unable to answer ambiguous questions like:

"Did the Red Sox win most of their games in July?"

The *baseball* program is one of a number of question-answering ones of which Winograd says: "Their restricted domain often allows them to use special purpose heuristics which achieve impressive results with a minimum of concern for the complexities of language."

Winograd's own work is still within a restricted domain (the space with cubes and pyramids, or *blocks world*), but it exemplifies methods having wider applicability.

WINOGRAD'S BLOCKS WORLD

Winograd's program[1] is named *SHRDLU*, the collection of letters being a codeword used by linotype operators and not the familiar acronym of computer jargon. Hofstadter[6], in his book which seeks, among other things, to connect recursion in programming with the music of Bach, has parodied the title of a Bach aria as "*SHRDLU* Toy of Man's Devising".

SHRDLU uses a language-analysis system called *PROGRAMMAR* to analyse its input. This combines semantic and syntactic features. As shown by the example "The old man's glasses were filled with sherry", an analysis system must be able to backtrack when it finds progress impossible on the basis of its current guesses. *PROGRAMMAR* allows for backtracking but, like a human, uses it only occasionally. Like the chess program of Botvinnik it has sufficiently powerful heuristics to let it make the right choice most of the time.

SHRDLU also uses a system termed *PLANNER* which is sometimes referred to as an extension of the programming language LISP (see Chapter 13). In fact, *PLANNER* provides much more than is usually expected of a programming language. It maintains a *database*, or *belief system*, in which assertions about the *blocks world* are stored.

Most of the assertions refer either to properties of objects or to relations between objects. Properties and relations are much the same sort of thing, except that a property refers to one object and a relation to more than one. In the formalism used to represent assertions in *PLANNER*, words denoting properties or relations are preceded by the sign # to distinguish them. The assertions "London is a city" and "James is the father of Alex" would be represented by:

(# CITY : LONDON)
(# FATHER OF : JAMES : ALEX)

Some of the relations can link three or more objects, and it is essential for the use of this formalism to know the appropriate number of objects for a given relation. The relation GIVE links three objects, so that "Harry gives (or gave) Alice the jewels" would be represented by:

(# GIVE : HARRY : ALICE : JEWELS)

The power of *PLANNER* is greatly extended by the fact that it can express properties of relations, and relations between relations. This is particularly useful in representing events, which, like the giving of jewels by Harry to Alice, can be represented as relations. They are relations having properties of time and place and possible relations depending on these.

A relation can be given a name to allow it to be referred to in other assertions. The name is placed after the list of objects to which the relation refers, so that the above relation can be labelled as REL2 by the form:

(# GIVE : HARRY : ALICE : JEWELS : REL2)

Winograd illustrates the possibilities by representing the sentence "Harry slept on the porch after he gave Alice the jewels" as follows:

(# SLEEP : HARRY : REL1)
(# LOCATION : REL1 : PORCH)
(# GIVE : HARRY : ALICE : JEWELS : REL2)
(# AFTER : REL1 : REL2)

PLANNER can accept assertions and adds them in this form to its database. It can also form consequences of the assertions it has. There is a certain problem of strategy here. When an addition is made to the database a scan can be made to see what fresh consequences are now possible. If they are all formed and added to the database, subsequent operations using the database are likely to be faster because these consequences never have to be derived again. On the other hand, the database could grow to an unmanageable size, so some selection is necessary. This is similar to the problem mentioned in Chapter 4 under *automated mathematics* of selecting "interesting" results.

In order to form consequences, *PLANNER* must have rules allowing the formation of new assertions from existing ones. This requires the introduction of *variables* and also of the *quantifiers* FORALL and EXISTS and the logical operators AND, OR, NOT and IMPLIES.

The assertion "All humans are fallible" or "That X is human implies X is fallible" would be represented as:

(FORALL(X) (IMPLIES (# HUMAN X) (# FALLIBLE X)))

An important difference between *PLANNER* and some other deductive systems is that *theorems* are represented by *procedures* — pieces of program allowing the theorem to be applied, by a call of the procedure, to some specific object. Winograd refers to the (facetious, it is to be hoped!) theorem stated as follows: A thesis is acceptable if either it is long or contains a persuasive argument.

The procedure representing this can be called to try to determine whether some given thesis is acceptable. Since the property of being long can probably be checked very simply by calling another procedure this is done first. If (and only if) the thesis is not long, the attempt must be made to decide whether it contains a persuasive argument. There is probably no single theorem which evaluates this, and the procedure contains an instruction which means "Search for theorems which reach conclusions about persuasive arguments, and try them until one is found which satisfies the requirement".

These other theorems may contain instructions of the "search" kind, so the problem-solving process can become complex. It can be represented as a tree search since each precedure can call any of a number of others. A procedure has to be called with reference to a suitable set of objects — in the above case to a specific thesis. Sometimes the operation ends in a report of failure; the above one must do so, if it is valid, for a thesis which is short and contains no persuasive argument.

The *PLANNER* language, in conjunction with its database, can answer questions of considerable complexity. The above indicates how it could answer the (suitably transformed) question "Is Sam's thesis acceptable?". Essentially the same arrangement allows the system to obey commands. A common type of command to *SHRDLU* is "Put object A onto object B". The procedure representing the theorem PUTON contains a series of instructions whose execution requires the calling of other theorems and may depend on searches. It is necessary to ensure that there is room for object A on top of object B, and then the top of object A must be cleared so that it can be picked up, and so on.

Finally, the required action, if it can be carried out at all, is represented in terms of the basic theorems MOVETO, GRASP and UNGRASP, which generate commands to the display system to alter the stored details of the *blocks world*. The action of MOVETO is to move a simulated hand, along with whatever it may be grasping, to a new location. GRASP causes it to pick up one object. UNGRASP causes release of the object, but fails if the object is not suitably supported.

Winograd quotes numerous examples of dialogue between *SHRDLU* and an experimenter (see also Hofstadter, pp. 586-593). The simple command:

"Pick up a big red block"

produces from *SHRDLU* the simple reply "OK" after the command has been obeyed. The state of the *blocks world* when the command was given was such that the big red block was supporting a green block, so *SHRDLU* had first to find a new place for this and to move it away.

SHRDLU also deals with pronoun references, as in response to the command:

"Find a block which is taller than the one you are holding and put it in the box."

To this, *SHRDLU* replies first:

"By 'it' I assume you mean the block which is taller than the one I am holding."

After making the moves according to this assumption, *SHRDLU* again responds with "OK".

SHRDLU can also answer quite complex questions, such as:

"How many blocks are not in the box?"

To this, *SHRDLU* answered, correctly, "Four of them", and was then asked:

"Is at least one of them narrower than the one I told you to pick up?"

To this last question *SHRDLU* again replies, correctly, "Yes, the red cube". This response is impressive, not only because of the complicated structure of the question but also because "one of them" only makes sense with reference to the previous question. Also, "the one I told you to pick up" is only interpreted by going even further back.

MENU-TYPE USE OF NATURAL LANGUAGE

It is perhaps worth emphasising that there are relatively trivial ways in which a program may be written so as to give the user a pleasant feeling of being involved in a natural-language dialogue. It is very easy to arrange that an interactive program asks questions of its user in natural language. The questions can be long and complicated provided the answers they invite come from a finite set of possibilities. A list of options can be presented as a self-explanatory "menu" from which the user makes a choice in a simple way, either by typing in a number or by moving a cursor to point to the chosen entry.

This is a technique familiar to users of interactive computing facilities, but is perhaps worth mentioning to make it clear that it is not necessary to implement something like *SHRDLU* to put a user in some sort of natural-language environment.

REFERENCES

1. T. Winograd, *Understanding Natural Language* (Edinburgh University Press, Edinburgh, 1973).
2. R.C. Shank, "Identification of conceptualizations underlying natural language" In: *Computer Models of Thought and Language* R.C. Shank (Ed) (Freeman, San Francisco, 1973) pp. 187-247.
3. I.D. Hill, "Wouldn't it be nice if we could write computer programs in ordinary English — or would it?" *Computer Bulletin* **16**, 306-312 (1972).
4. F.G. Duncan, "Our ultimate metalanguage: an after-dinner talk"

In: *Formal Language Description Languages for Computer Programming* T.B. Steel (Ed) (North Holland, Amsterdam, 1966).

5. B.F. Green, A.K. Wolf, C. Chomsky and K. Laughery, "Baseball: an automatic question answerer" In: *Computers and Thought* E.A. Feigenbaum and J. Feldman (Ed) (McGraw-Hill, New York, 1963) pp. 207-216.

6. D.R. Hofstadter, *Gödel, Escher, Bach: An Eternal Golden Braid* (Penguin Books, Harmondsworth, 1980).

Chapter 10

TWO IMPORTANT APPLICATION AREAS

One of the motivations for A.I. studies is the possibility of exploiting the new techniques for practical purposes. The present period of financial stringency has increased the emphasis on projects having relatively short-term practical value, but is not the only reason for interest in them.

Practical applications of pattern-recognition techniques have already been mentioned; reading machines are of great value commercially and could be to blind people, and there are various applications for speech recognition even when restricted to a small vocabulary.

In this chapter two other application areas will be discussed, namely those of *Robotics* and of *Expert Systems*.

ROBOTICS

Robotics is the area of study aimed at bringing computers out into the real world. Modern machines have been contrasted with the relatively brute-force ones of the Industrial Revolution, but in robotics they are required to have muscles as well as intelligence. They are also required to obtain their inputs by "eyes" and "ears" (some schemes going beyond the capabilities of human vision by using laser techniques and hence a range-finding capacity much more accurate than is allowed by human stereoscopic vision). *Scene analysis* is essential for advanced work in robotics.

Many of the things people do with apparent ease prove to be very difficult for machines. As one writer has put it, crossing a moderately busy street without mishap is a small step for a man but one which has not been taken by an unaided computer. Although computer programs have appeared to be poised to make original contributions to mathematics, it is very difficult to write one to control a robot to go round a house and empty the ash-trays. Clearly, the way that tasks must be ranked in order of difficulty for humans is different from the ranking according to difficulty for machines.

Although Winograd's principal motivation in his work (Chapter 9) was to study natural-language understanding, his choice of the *blocks world* as a universe of discourse was prompted by appreciation of the importance of robotics. Of course, by operating in a simulated blocks world he avoided the need to consider scene analysis. Other work at the Massachusetts Institute of Technology has allowed the manipulation of real blocks and has required attention to both scene analysis and the command of real manipulators.

Even the design of manipulators is a matter of some complexity. People are able to pick up fragile objects like eggs, usually without crushing them. Also, without conscious attention to the matter they apply much greater pressure when required to pick up a heavy smooth-sided object. The action probably depends on detection of very slight deformations of the object being grasped, so that its resistance to crushing may be estimated.

The possibility of a robot table-tennis player has received consideration but has not been seriously tackled as a project. The reason seems to be that the amount of computing power needed to make the necessary decisions in the time available, is beyond current resources. As in other areas of A.I., the attempt to simulate human intelligence inspires respect for it.

THE NEED FOR ROBOTS

One of the uses people would like to make of robots is to send them to places which are dangerous for humans. They can be useful in exploring distant planets, or carrying out operations deep in the ocean. These could be concerned with salvage or, at lesser depths, with farming, or with prospecting for oil and other minerals and the procurement of the minerals when found. Other dangerous environments in which robots

can be useful arise because of fire, radioactivity, explosion and ava-
lanche danger, etc.

It can also be useful to send robots to locations which are not only
dangerous for humans but physically impossible. One example would
be the surface of a planet with gravity much greater than on earth.
Other examples arise where a person's size debars him; robots could
make inspections and repairs inside pipelines (in simple ways they
already do), and could be passed through the throat and other orifices
of patients to perform surgical operations without the need to penetrate
the skin.

Apart from these, many of the things we would like to have robots do
are things we do not want to do ourselves because we find them tedious
and want to spend our time doing something else. An electronic
housemaid to empty the ashtrays and to do other chores would relieve
tedium, as would an electronic gardener. It is likely, though, that robots
will become economically viable in industry before they are commonly
found in domestic service,

INDUSTRIAL ROBOTICS

Many of the tasks carried out manually in present-day industry could
currently be automated. To identify all the reasons for not automating
them would be difficult and outside the scope of the present discussion.
Simple inertia on the part of management is undoubtedly one contributing factor, and so is opposition from workers and trade unions
and worry about the unemployment which could result from large-scale
automation. (With regard to the last point, it *should* be possible to find
a way of organizing society so that a reasonably equitable division of
necessities and luxuries of life is not conditional on the continuance of
inefficient methods of production.)

Apart from these considerations, however, a very good reason for
managers to be wary of automation is that the standard techniques are
inflexible. A substantial investment must be made in specialised
machinery, perhaps with some of it specially developed for the application. No manager wants to make this investment and to find, a short
time later, that what he is equipped to produce is no longer wanted.
This can happen because of a change in fashion or a technical development making the product obsolete.

The nightmare prospect of a specialised assembly line designed for an unwanted product makes managers inclined to stick with human workers using less sophisticated machines. The factory, or part of it, can then be rearranged fairly quickly to make something different. Also, human operators show flexibility in not requiring their input of raw material (components to be assembled, say) to arrive with a standard orientation ensured perhaps by mounting on pallets or packing into magazines. One way of arranging for standard orientation in an automated factory is to have a tightly-coupled production line in which each process feeds straight into the next. This is not a good solution because the breakdown of one machine brings the whole line to a halt. With human operators it is possible to have stocks of part-finished items which allow, for a time, continuous operation of the stages of production before and ahead of the interrupted one.

The aim of work on industrial robotics is to produce machines having flexibility approaching that of human operators. Using scene analysis techniques, robot devices have been able to assemble mechanisms from components dumped in a pile on the bench, just as a human fitter would do. Michie[1] has described such a robot developed in Edinburgh, and work is in progress in many other places. The Edinburgh robot also has flexibility in that it can be retrained to perform a different assembly task.

Not all of the operations of industry require the sophisticated cognitive abilities of the Edinburgh robot. Many tasks could be performed by a "blind" robot, perhaps with simple sensors to ensure that a workpiece or other raw material is in place before it starts its sequence of operations. Such robots can sometimes be retrained for a new task simply by being made to go through the new sequence of operations under manual control. Robots capable of being trained in this way for paint-spraying are now well known; paint-spraying is of course a task requiring less precision of movement than do many other industrial operations.

LIMITATIONS

The Edinburgh robot is one of many advanced cognitive problem-solving systems. Another interesting one has been termed "Shakey" at the Stanford Research Institute (Stanford, California). It is self-propelling and communicates by radio with the computer which is its "brain". It moves around in a suite of rooms and keeps track of its own position in them by a system of dead-reckoning periodically corrected by taking "fixes" on landmarks such as corners of rooms. It can see and identify objects in the rooms and adds them to its internal model. It can be given an instruction like "push the cube which is in room 2 into room 4", and it will plan a route avoiding known obstacles so as to achieve this goal. If it meets new obstacles on the way the plan is modified accordingly.

All these systems lend themselves to impressive demonstrations which are shown on films at A.I. conferences. Although their problem-solving powers are impressive, they generally operate very slowly. Most practical applications will demand faster responses, and it seems there is a need for much improvement in computational efficiency before these *advanced* cognitive systems are widely utilised. On the other hand, robots of a lower level of sophistication are being employed in ever-increasing numbers.

Even in the seemingly-simple matter of controlling a jointed limb there are tricky computational problems. For a limb like the human arm, the moment of inertia of what has to be rotated about the shoulder joint is strongly dependent on the angle of the elbow-joint, being much greater when the elbow is extended than when it is flexed. Information on elbow-flexion is available within the control system and could usefully modify the commands to the shoulder muscles. In the nervous system the complex calculations needed for this are actually performed[2]. On the other hand, current artificial systems for controlling multi-jointed limbs operate by the relatively inefficient brute-force method of using "stiff" servomechanisms at each joint to control the movements irrespective, within limits, of the moments of inertia.

The control of complex patterns of activity such as walking introduces special problems. A form of hierarchical operation is needed, with the general pattern of movements being decided at a high level, and the details being filled in at lower levels. There is a great deal of evidence that biological control has this character; the motor cortex of the brain issues commands for movements, not for contractions of individual muscles. Physiologists have used the term *synergy* for the pattern of muscular activity corresponding to a higher-level command, and the design of artificial walking systems requires the implementation of *synergies*.

These hierarchical-control aspects have received particular attention in the design of a six-legged walking robot[3], which is of as much interest from a neurophysiological as from an industrial point of view.

The use of *synergies* to reduce the degrees of freedom of a control task is important in another area of application connected with robotics. It is important in the design of prosthetic limbs to replace missing real ones. The physiologist V.S. Gurfinkel who was concerned with the walking robot has also been concerned with prosthesis.

ROBOTS AND ECOLOGY

Consideration of environmental problems[4] shows there are some areas in which robotics techniques could be vital. Modern agricultural methods require large amounts of energy[5]. Blaxter[6] has shown that the energy required to grow a crop of potatoes (including that used in fertilizer manufacture) is only a very little short of the energy content of the peeled potatoes. The fact that peasant communities have been able to nourish themselves largely by growing potatoes in the old-fashioned way shows that it is possible to keep the energy expenditure much lower. Blaxter discusses some ways in which economies could be achieved; fertilizers could be produced in other ways, and there are low-energy alternatives to ploughing.

However, one of the main differences between traditional and modern agricultural methods is in their use of information. A man digging potatoes infers from the upper part of the plant where the potatoes are likely to be and after turning the earth he spots them visually. A harvesting machine, on the other hand, stirs the soil in an energy-expensive way because it does not see where the potatoes are.

One way in which the human race could adapt to the scarcity of fossil fuel would be by returning (those of us who have left it, that is) to a primitive way of life in which agricultural operations are done in old-fashioned ways. Some enthusiasts would argue that we would all be more healthy and happier if we did. On the other hand, not all of the time saved by automation is squandered pointlessly; it is also devoted to a multitude of cultural and intellectual pursuits which are generally regarded as essential features of civilisation. The use of robotic devices in agriculture and elsewhere may allow these to be preserved while still growing food with low energy expenditure. The information processing on which the energy conservation depends would then be done electronically rather than by human nervous systems.

Robotic devices could also play a large part in the recycling of waste materials. At present old motor cars, for example, are often squeezed into one block of scrap steel, after removal of the battery and incineration of everything that will burn. In view of the special alloys and other materials which go into a car this is extremely wasteful, and yet it is not economic to separate the parts for individual recycling. The use of robots to dismantle the cars in spite of the variability from one to the next is probably the only feasible solution. One of the main uses of cognitive robots may come to be in what the dustmen call "totting".

There are other environmental problems which could be partially solved by the use of robots. Weedkillers of a particular type are causing concern because of their long-term effect on the soil; their use could be avoided if robots, capable of distinguishing weeds from crop plants, could be set to dig out the weeds. Insecticides are open to objections on environmental grounds; in some cases an alternative way of dealing with an insect pest would be to let robots perform what gardeners euphemistically term "finger-and-thumb" work on the larvae. In areas where water is scarce, the use of robots to estimate the water requirements of individual plants from their appearance, and to make application accordingly, would allow the best possible use of the water available.

Naturally, the range of applications of cognitive robots depends on how cheaply they can be built and operated. The cost of electronic circuitry continues to fall, and the power requirements of solid-state devices are very low. At the same time, the rewards for solving environmental problems continually grow. The situation may be summed up by saying that the methods for saving human effort, initiated in the Industrial Revolution, are methods which make little use of information processing. Many of them are wasteful of energy or have other bad side-effects, because of their block-buster nature. They become increasingly untenable as resources become exhausted or contaminated. A return to information-intensive methods requires either that people do much more manual work or that robots do it.

EXPERT SYSTEMS

In fairly recent years, computer programs termed *expert systems*[7] have been written with reference to many different areas of expertise. Diagnosis in various areas of medicine has received particular attention, and so have topics concerned with management, oil and mineral exploration, income tax, work scheduling and technological problems of various kinds. Programs purporting to be expert systems for some of these areas are being made available commercially, some of them running on mini-computers.

An expert system is intended to embody a substantial part of the knowledge of a human expert in the particular field, and to be able to utilise this stored knowledge as the human would. For instance, an expert system in the medical field is able to perform diagnosis — the patient's symptoms are put in as data and the program reaches conclusions about possible diseases.

There have been many attempts to develop programs for medical diagnosis before the emergence of those now referred to as expert systems. Some of the earlier systems were found to be of value as an aid to a doctor, but only to about the same extent as a well-cross-referenced record of his past cases. A program termed *MYCIN* (and another developed from it called *TEIRESIAS*), originating in Stanford University, came to be accepted as aids to diagnosis of a much superior sort. They have in fact come to be accepted with enthusiasm by medical practitioners. One of the reasons for their success is that they model inexact reasoning. That is to say, the data base includes representations of rules like "If .... then there is a suggestion of ...." and these are used in diagnosis.

For use by the program, the rule is expressed a little more precisely, with a numerical estimate of the probability of the conclusion. What a human thinks of as "a suggestion of" might be represented as probability 0.1. What a person thinks of as "probably" might be given the value 0.8, and so on. The program can derive a number of alternative diagnoses, with associated probability estimates.

An important feature of such a program is that its database be capable of expansion (or correction) as new research results become known. The programs can also indicate what further observations or tests would reduce the uncertainty, and they hold information on the cost as well as the usefulness of the different tests. This is "cost" in a wide sense, including not only financial cost but also the danger, unpleasantness and inconvenience for the patient. The system favours tests which are cheap, safe and painless.

In *MYCIN* the database entries are mainly of the simple conditional form:

"If .... then .... with probability ...."

in which "then" is followed by a factual statement about the patient's condition. (In the original application of *MYCIN* to identification of infectious diseases the statement would refer to types of organism which could be the cause of the disease.)

The database entries for *TEIRESIAS* are similar to those for *MYCIN*, but allowance is made for rules to govern the strategy of search through the rules, as well as for rules making factual assertions. The entry which follows "then" in a *TEIRESIAS* rule may be to the effect that, in searching for rules which mention certain relevant topics, the search for rules mentioning a topic A should take priority over the search for rules mentioning topic B. This gives the search method some similarity to the methods embodied in *PLANNER* as described in Chapter 9.

A feature of these programs which was essential to their success was the facility they embodied for being able to explain, in an approximation to conversational English, just how any decision was arrived at. This was done by making the program keep a "trace" or record of the steps it had taken. They can even be challenged by questions like "Why didn't you consider ....?" and will explain how some possibility was eliminated from consideration.

The "explain" facility was necessary to allow these methods to gain acceptance by medical practitioners. It has also proved useful in developing the database to correspond as closely as possible to the methods of the human expert. Where the diagnosis produced by the program differed from that of the expert, he was asked to work through the steps by which he had reached his decision. The "explain" facility made it possible to compare his chain of deduction with that of the program and to identify the point at which a discrepancy arose. This would indicate a needed amendment to the rules in the data base.

The ultimate responsibility for medical decisions rests with the physician, and the use of a computer program could be held to be unethical if it did not have the "explain" facility. With this, however, the physician can satisfy himself of the validity of all the reasoning and there is no question of irresponsibility. There is a good deal of evidence that he is a much better physician with the computer than without it.

REFERENCES

1. D. Michie, *On Machine Intelligence* (Edinburgh University Press, Edinburgh, 1974).
2. M. Benati, S. Gaglio, P. Morasso, V. Tagliasco and R. Zaccoria, "Anthropomorphic robotics" *Biological Cybernetics* **38**, 125-140 and 141-150 (1980).
3. V.S. Gurfinkel, E.V. Gurfinkel, A.Yu. Shneider, E.A. Devjanin, A.V. Lensky and L.G. Shtilman, "Walking robot with supervisory control" *Mechanism and Machine Theory* **16**, 31-36 (1981).
4. A.M. Andrew, "Why robotics?" *Kybernetes* **4**, 2-8 (1975).
5. D. Pimentel, "Food and the energy crisis" *Agricult. Engin.* **54**, No. 12, p. 11 (1973).
6. K. Blaxter, "Power and agricutural revolution" *New Scientist* **61**, 400-403 (Feb. 14, 1974).
7. E.A. Feigenbaum, "Themes and case studies of knowledge engineering," In: *Expert Systems in the Microelectronics Age* D. Michie (Ed) (Edinburgh University Press, Edinburgh, 1979) pp. 3-25.

Chapter 11

AESTHETICS

Computers find a variety of applications related to artistic pursuits. In most of these the computer is merely a tool of the artist, perhaps a revolutionary one but still a tool. However, there has also been interest in programming computers to create original artistic works, both in the area of visual art and in music. Computer programs have also been made to write poetry, but probably not with the expectation of producing serious work.

In this area, machine "intelligence" is even more nebulous than in the others which have been considered, since no one can define a "work of art" in objective terms. The only possible definition is as something which evokes a feeling of pleasure in a human listener or observer, and the stronger the feeling the better the work of art. Since humans have, by this definition, a built-in means of assessing the quality of a putative work of art it seems unlikely that machines can ever rival human performance in artistic creation.

The incorporation of a corresponding facility in a computer program must depend on some analysis or hypothesis about the nature of aesthetic experience. Although the ultimate criterion can only be assessed by humans, criteria derived from such analysis or hypothesis can be of value. Within some restricted field a computer program can appear to know, better than we do ourselves, what we like. Ultimately, it cannot "know better", but it can represent human preferences in a way that allows prompt and consistent responses and thus gives heuristic guidance in the production of new works.

Statistical analysis of existing, accepted, works may allow conclusions about their necessary properties. New works can then be generated conforming to the statistically-determined rules and using a pseudo-random number generator (Appendix 2 of Chapter 1) to give variations within the constraints. The generation of computer music follows this general pattern.

A hypothesis about the nature of aesthetic experience has been made by Pask[1] as follows:

"Man is prone to seek novelty in his environment and, having found a novel situation, to learn how to control it. Let us develop and qualify this cybernetic statement. In the symbolic domain which constitutes the most important aspect of the human environment, 'novelty' inheres in events or configurations that appear ambiguous to a given individual, that engender uncertainty with respect to his present state of knowing and pose problems. 'Control', in this symbolic domain, is broadly equivalent to 'problem solving' but it may also be read as 'coming to terms with' or 'explaining' or 'relating to an existing body of experience'. Further, when learning to control or to solve problems man necessarily conceptualizes and abstracts. Because of this, the human environment is interpreted at various levels in an hierarchy of abstraction (on the same page we see letters, words, grammatical sentences and beautiful prose). These propensities are at the root of curiosity and the assimilation of knowledge. They impel man to explore, discover and explain his inanimate surroundings. Addressed to the social environment of other men, they lead him into social communication, conversation and other modes of partially co-operative interaction.

To summarise the issue in slightly different words, man is always aiming to achieve some goal and he is always looking for new goals. Commonly, he deals with goals at several levels of an hierarchical structure in which some members are freshly formulated and some are in the process of formulation. My contention is that man enjoys performing these jointly innovative and cohesive operations. Together, they represent an essentially human and inherently pleasurable mode of activity."

Aesthetic experience is here seen as the exploration of suitably complex novel environments and the discovery of structure and significance in them. Starting from some such model or rationalisation of aesthetic experience, computer programs (or special-purpose electronic circuitry as described by Pask in the same paper) can be devised to generate "works of art" satisfying the requirements implied by the model. Gordon Pask gives an account of a "Musicolour" system which created visual displays automatically synchronised to music and allowing audience interaction. (Simpler systems producing "light shows" with synchronisation are now commonplace; the work of Pask and his colleagues was of a pioneering nature.)

Important though aesthetic experience is in human life, it is difficult to explain its evolutionary emergence. Viewed in terms of the above it would seem to be closely allied to curiosity. Curiosity has survival value (despite the proberb "Curiosity killed the cat"); it is a manifestation of the heuristic principle that it is a good thing to acquire information about the environment even when it has no immediate payoff.

However, the type of exploration inherent in aesthetic experience does not have obvious survival value, unless by virtue of improving the person's exploratory abilities through practice. It looks like a spurious off-short of curiosity — one might even say curiosity "gone wrong". If it is permissible to view aesthetic experience in this way (which seems presumptuous and Philistine, although logical), it would be reasonable to suppose that machines could evolve a different kind of "aesthetic experience" as an off-shoot of some heuristic found by them to be useful. Unless the machines were highly autonomous such a development would be seen by a programmer as nothing more than a heuristic "gone wrong" and would be eliminated forthwith.

VISUAL ART

As a tool, the computer plays an important part in visual art. Existing programs can be given data specifying the shape of proposed designs for objects such as buildings or motor cars or items of furniture. A picture of the object is shown on a screen, and the program can be instructed to alter the assumed viewpoint, so that the object is seen rotating into different positions. This is, of course, a valuable facility for designers.

A computer-generated moving display has been used as an aid to choreography. Stylised representations of ballet dancers were shown moving, as though in three dimensions, on a representation of a stage.

Computer methods are used in the animation of cartoon films. Many computers are equipped with facilities for graphical input as well as graphical output on a screen and/or plotter. It is often arranged that pictures can be drawn on the graphical input medium (which may be the screen itself, using a "light pen") and stored and made to appear on the screen. If the display allows colour, it is sometimes arranged that a part of the input area is effectively an artist's palette with blobs of different colours of "paint". Applying the light pen (or other form of cursor) to a colour blob in the palette area causes it to commence making a trace in that colour.

In its simple form, colour graphics with a "palette" gives an artist a facility similar to what he has with a paint brush and a real palette. In computer graphics, however, he can have additional facilities which are certainly not available to traditional artists. He can, for instance, draw a line and then press a button to indicate that it is meant to be a straight line, and immediately it becomes so. He can call in other modes of operation to shift the ends of the line to new positions, the line remaining straight and shifting accordingly, or to move whole sections of his picture from one location on the screen to another.

Graphic communication with computers has innumerable applications in science and technology. Programmers often feel a certain aesthetic excitement when writing programs to produce graphic output. Many of the pictures which arise in technical and scientific contexts are extremely attractive — families of mathematical curves, perspective representations of three-dimensional graphs, Lissajous figures, molecular structures, exploded views of mechanisms, and so on. Not surprisingly, there is interest in the use of computer graphics to produce pictures purely for their aesthetic value.

In most of this work the picture is not specified in detail by the programmer; the program is to some extent creative since the picture is partly determined by pseudo-random numbers.

Fig. 11.1 shows the result of generating a sequence of 30 points within a square, the x- and y-coordinates of each point being pseudo-random selections from a uniform distribution. The points are joined by straight lines in the sequence of their generation and the last point is joined to the first. A figure with as little structure as this is not usually thought to be very interesting; a slightly more interesting one is formed by arranging that the chosen points are not uniformly distributed. In Fig. 11.2, the method of generation is such that the points are more likely to fall in one particular quadrant of the square than elsewhere, and the effect is somewhat more pleasing.

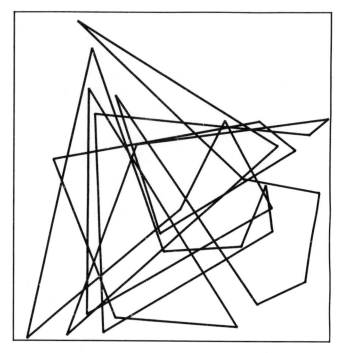

Fig. 11.1. Picture formed by choosing 30 points in a square, each being joined to the next and the last to the first. The distribution over the square is uniform.

Most computer art has a good deal more structure than these figures show. A well-known picture termed *Gravel Stones* by Georg Nees[2] has rows of squares which are regular at the top of the picture but become increasingly disordered towards the bottom. The effect is obtained by using a pseudo-random number generator to determine the displacements of the squares, and multiplying its outputs by numbers proportional to the distance from the top of the picture of the squares on which they will be used.

The disturbances of the squares can be in size, orientation and position (if desired, vertical and horizontal disturbances in position could be introduced separately). Nees allows disturbance of orientation and position and achieves a striking effect.

Figs. 11.3 to 11.7 show pictures similar to *Gravel Stones* but having a much smaller array of squares. Several of the possible combinations of the three types of disturbance are introduced and produce interesting effects.

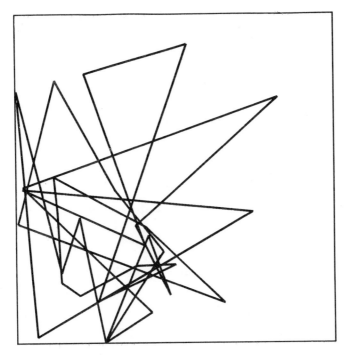

Fig. 11.2. Picture like Fig. 11.1 but with a higher density of points in one quadrant of the square than in the rest. For each point, a pseudo-random equiprobable choice was made as to whether the selection would be from the lower left-hand quadrant or from the whole square. Since the quadrant includes one fourth of the total area, the expected density of points in it is five times that in the other three quadrants.

MUSIC

The automatic composition of music is visualised in both of the famous gloomy predictions of man's future, namely Aldous Huxley's *Brave New World* and George Orwell's *Nineteen Eighty Four*. In both of these the music was aimed at the intellectually inferior sections of the community, namely the "epsilons" and "proles" in the respective works.

Not all approaches to music composition have such unfortunate connotations. Scholes[3] refers to a number of early attempts at mechanical composition, one of them due to Samuel Pepys and still to be seen in the Pepysian Museum at Magdalene College, Cambridge. Another dating from 1824 and termed a "Componium" is referred to by both Scholes and Gabor[4] and is preserved in Brussels.

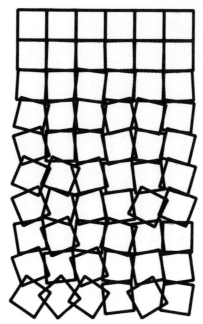

Fig. 11.3. Array of squares, with pseudo-random disturbance whose magnitude increases from top to bottom. Here the disturbance is of orientation only.

Fig. 11.4. As Fig. 11.3, but with disturbance of position only.

Fig. 11.5. As last two Figures, but combining disturbance of orientation and position. This corresponds to *Gravel Stones* by Georg Nees.

Fig. 11.6. As foregoing Figures, with disturbance of size and orientation.

Fig. 11.7.   As foregoing Figures, with all three types of disturbance.

Another system for automatic composition was described in a pamphlet which attributed it to Mozart. The method depends on throwing dice. Some writers have taken the alleged authorship seriously, but Scholes is scornful of it.

What is probably the most famous work on music composition is that of Hiller[5] who combined the results of a number of experiments into a work called the *Illiac Suite* (ILLIAC being the name of a computer in the University of Illinois). As might be expected, the reactions of listeners to this unusual music are mixed, but it is usually accepted as non-trivial. The fact that it is performed by human players (a string quartette) leaves room for suspicion that something is added in the playing. This would be what musicians call "interpretation" though just what is being "interpreted" in this case is difficult to say.

Some later ideas on the use of computers to compose and modify music, and to synthesise musical sounds, can be found in a book edited by von Foerster and Beauchamp[6].

POETRY

In Appendix 3 of Chapter 13, a method is outlined for generating grammatical sentences pseudo-randomly. When this is used with a fairly
large vocabulary (the *terminal symbols* of the syntax rules), the
vocabulary consisting of suitably flowery and emotive words, the output has the character of modern poetry. It has to be termed "modern"
because (a) it is enigmatic and (b) it does not rhyme.

In a light-hearted investigation[7] of the possibilities two research
students set up the method with a vocabulary of between 50 and 100
words. They published the following example of output. (They are not
explicit as to whether this represents consecutively-generated material
or is selected and assembled from a greater amount of output.) Some of
the sentences are such that a human poet might have been proud to have
thought of them:

Limp hope calls at moon

Stone calls love while limp stark longing becomes strange
but icy tree pushes with despair

Brightness becomes misty

Stone stands silken as stark silk stands bright from
silken green sun night
though bank becomes bright
but strange brightness stands limp
though love stands misty with limp green crystal
but love calls slowly at earth strange with longing

Fire becomes silken while hope caresses slowly as misty
misty snow

THE VALUE OF COMPUTER ART

In view of what was said earlier about the nature of aesthetic experience, this is not an area in which one should look for a high level of
"pure" Artificial Intelligence. Good results must depend on the interaction of machine and programmer. In visual art some very interesting
and pleasing results have been obtained by such interaction.

Even when the results are far from being world-shattering as works of art, work on computer composition can be useful as a means of studying the nature of aesthetics. As mentioned earlier, guide-lines for the generation of "works of art" can be derived by statistical analysis or on the basis of a theory such as that of Pask. Computer composition provides a means of testing the degree to which a particular set of guidelines is adequate to ensure acceptable results. This indicates the extent to which the guide-lines embody the essence of artistry.

Computer composition also allows experiments in combining randomness and structure in different proportions. This applies to both visual art and to music. A highly-random picture like Fig. 11.1 is not very interesting, and neither is random music. Computer composition allows randomness and regularity to be combined in a controllable and quantifiable way.

Computer-generated material often has an attractive freedom from the triteness which tends to mar the compositions (whether literary, visual or musical) of non-expert humans. This is presumably because humans cannot help trying to embody structure and "meaning" in what they produce, and often embody something trivial. This is actually one respect in which machines show superiority over many humans. Whether it is superiority in any deep sense is debatable — it is possible that the freedom from triteness is attractive because the listener (or viewer) assumes the absence of trivial regularities to betoken some profound "meaning". If this is so, continued exposure to computer-composed material could produce disillusionment. These general issues are discussed in various papers in Reichardt's book[8].

REFERENCES

1. G. Pask, "A comment, a case history and a plan" *Cybernetics, Art and Ideas* pp. 76-99 (See Ref. 8).

2. H.W. Franke, *Computer Graphics, Computer Art* (Phaidon Press, London, 1971). *Gravel Stones* by Georg Nees is reproduced on p. 30.

3. P.A. Scholes, *The Oxford Companion to Music* (Oxford University Press, London, 7th ed 1947) pp. 204-205, and illustrations facing pages 181 and 194.

4. D. Gabor, "Technological civilization and man's future" *Cybernetics, Art and Ideas* 18-24 (See Ref. 8).

5. L.A. Hiller and R. Baker, "Computer music" *Computer Applications in the Behavioural Sciences* H. Borko (Ed) (Prentice Hall, Englewood Cliffs, N.J., 1962) Ch. 18, pp. 424-451.

6. H. von Foerster and J.W. Beauchamp (Eds) *Music by Computers* (Wiley, New York, 1969).

7. T.G. Swann, E. Drawneek and PDP8, "Bridging the emotion gap; a proposition" *Research ?* (Physics Dept., University of Reading) February issue, pp. 28-29 (1970).

8. J. Reichardt, *Cybernetics, Art and Ideas* (Studio Vista, London, 1971).

Chapter 12

THE COMPETITION — REAL NEURONS

In all discussions of A.I. topics, the results achieved are compared with what brains achieve using real neurons. In most areas of A.I. endeavour the brain wins by a very comfortable margin, as will be seen from the summing-up in the next three chapters. Of course, this superiority is in the context of tasks in the A.I. field, which are pre-selected to be those which are difficult for machines though possible for brains.

Machines are superior to brains at what is termed "number-crunching" and other tasks (such as exhaustive searches) which can be precisely specified but require much computing effort. If, as seems likely, a computer is programmed soon to play virtually-unbeatable chess, the result will have been achieved by exploiting the enormous computational power of the machine rather than by imitating human methods.

Although the aim of this book is to discuss Artificial Intelligence, it is worth while to give some attention to the real neurons which underlie natural intelligence and to some aspects of their organisation. Some of these aspects are of particular interest from an A.I. point of view because of parallels which can be drawn between them and artificial systems.

Nerve cells are of microscopic size, the main "cell body" being typically about 30 microns across (where one micron is a millionth part of a metre, or a thousandth part of a millimetre). There are usually a great many outgrowths, or "processes" from the cell body. Most of these are branching structures called *dendrites*, running to perhaps 200 or 300

microns from the cell body. Most neurons have another outgrowth called the axon, whose length may be anything from 50 microns to several
metres. It often has many branches.

The nerve trunks or simply "nerves" of the body consist of bundles
of nerve fibres enclosed in a protective sheath, rather like an
underground telephone cable. The fibres are in fact axons of nerve cells
and they convey *nerve impulses.*

The whole nerve cell, including the dendrites and axon, is enclosed in
a membrane, and the chemical composition of the protoplasm inside
differs from that of the body fluid outside. The main difference is that
the interior is rich in potassium while the outside is rich in sodium. The
difference is maintained by a property of the membrane termed the
"sodium pump" and it results in an electrical potential difference
across the membrane. The inside of a resting neuron is about 70 mV
negative with respect to the outside.

If a small area of membrane becomes depolarised — i.e. comes not to
have the 70 mV potential difference across it — its permeability properties change in such a way that a current flows which affects neighbour-
ing areas and causes them to become depolarised too. The depolarisation is transient and the membrane returns to its resting state in about a
millisecond. The overall effect is such that, once a small area of the cell
body has become depolarised, a wave of depolarisation spreads over it
and runs right along the axon. The wave takes about a millisecond to
pass any one point. This is the propagated nerve impulse on which
nervous-system communication depends.

Some nerve fibres are covered with a layer of a fatty substance called
myelin and others are not. The larger the fibre the faster it conducts,
and transmission is much faster in myelinated fibres than in unmyelinated ones of the same size. (This seems to be due to the fact that
myelinated ones have small gaps every few millimetres, called "nodes of
Ranvier" and the excitation jumps from node to node.) The actual
velocities are slow compared to the transmission of electrical signals in
cables; a myelinated fibre conducts at a few tens of metres per second, a
value of a hundred metres per second being about the upper limit. For
small unmyelinated fibres speeds as low as a few tens of centimetres per
second have been quoted for components of the frog optic nerve.

The *axon* is the output signal pathway of the neuron. The cell body
and its dendrites have points (which may be as many as 10,000 on a
single neuron) at which the axons of other neurons can exert an in-

fluence. These points are termed *synapses* and they may be *excitatory* (tending to produce depolarisation of the neuron) or inhibitory (making it more difficult for the neuron to be excited, i.e. depolarised, by the effect of other neurons operating through excitatory synapses). Transmission across synapses is chemical in nature, a variety of *transmitter substances* being effective in different synapses.

A neuron, then, can be triggered to "fire" and produce an output impulse transmitted along its axon. The "firing" is normally produced by an impulse or impulses in the neurons which influence this one through excitatory synapses. Between the arrival of the input impulses and the appearance of the output one there is always a delay referred to as the *synaptic delay*, and it is about one millisecond.

The computing elements of the brain are therefore extremely slow compared to those of digital computers, whose speeds are now often quoted in nanoseconds (thousand-millionths of seconds). The very respectable computing power of the brain is achieved, not by high speed of operation at the neuronal level but by having many neurons active at the same time. This is in contrast to digital computers which are essentially serial in operation.

Although the brain, and the rest of the nervous system, are organised very differently from a digital computer, some aspects of their operation can be examined in much the same way as a piece of electronic equipment would be examined. The passage of a nerve impulse creates an electrical disturbance which can be detected by a small electrode near the nerve body or fibre. Very small electrodes, termed *microelectrodes*, have been made, and when these are carefully positioned with the help of a micrometer head, the signals in a single neuron can be picked up and amplified and recorded.

Microelectrodes have been made in various ways. The very finest are micro-pipettes — glass tubing drawn to a fine tip and filled with a conducting solution. Some have a tip diameter a small fraction of a micron, and these can penetrate the membrane of a neuron, apparently without affecting its operation. With a suitable high-impedance direct-coupled amplifier it is then possible to verify the potential difference of 70 mV across the membrane (a *very* high-impedance amplifier since the electrode resistance can be in excess of 100 Megohms). For other work electrodes which are not so fine are used; these do not penetrate the cells but with careful positioning they can produce single-unit records. They may be micro-pipettes or may consist of glass drawn down on to a fine platinum wire. There is another technique which depends on bringing tungsten wires to a fine point by electrolytic etching and then insulating almost to the tip with a thermosetting varnish.

It is also possible to excite neurons, and to initiate an impulse at any point along an axon, by applying a brief pulse of electic current (even though the normal means of excitation, through synaptic connections, is chemical). It is therefore possible to "tap in" to the nervous system of an animal, both to introduce signals into it and to record what is going on. (In experiments on the nervous system the animal is usually lightly anaesthetised — it has to be lightly because anaesthetics achieve their effect by influencing the nervous system. Where the aim is to study some part of the system other than the brain the animal may be *decerebrate* — that is to say, having had most of its brain removed under anaesthesia, the anaesthetic then being discontinued. There are also techniques for inserting a microelectrode into an animal's brain while it is anaesthetised, so as to allow subsequent recording or stimulation while the animal is conscious and unrestrained and apparently unperturbed.)

The nervous system has been very extensively studied and no attempt will be made here to review the. whole of neurophysiology. An admirable and thought-provoking attempt at such a review is the recent book by Sommerhoff[1]. Although a great deal is known there is also a great deal which is still highly mysterious. Two topics of particular relevance to A.I. will be discussed here, namely the neurophysiology of vision, and neural plasticity.

FROG VISION

In studies of the visual systems of animals a fairly coherent "story" has emerged, giving some insight into the early stages of visual-information processing. The eye is essentially a camera, with a lens focussing the image on to the retina, which is an array of a great many light-sensitive elements. In the human eye the number of primary receptors is over one hundred million (about 120,000,000 rods and 7,000,000 cones). In early work on the visual system it tended to be assumed that the outputs of these receptors were transmitted through the optic nerve for analysis by the brain, much in the way a television engineer would specify if he were prevented from using scanning to compress the picture into one high-bandwidth channel.

However, the picture cannot be transmitted to the brain exactly as received, because there are not enough fibres in the optic nerve. Each human optic nerve contains about one million fibres, so the image has to be condensed for transmission. The retina has a great deal of neural "circuitry" between the primary receptors and the *ganglion cells* whose axons are the fibres of the optic nerve, and the compression must take place there.

A study of the visual system of the frog by Lettvin and others[2] (including Andrew — see footnote to the paper by Lettvin *et al*) showed the frog retina to be operating in a way that would hardly have occurred to a television engineer. The frog retina has about a million primary receptors and half a million fibres in each optic nerve. These fibres, or "units" were found to belong to four classes, each responding in a way which could be related to the frog's way of life. They also map each retina on to the surface of the opposite-side optic lobe of the frog's brain, as a television engineer might expect. However, the nature of the four types of unit is such that it seems the visual image is already being processed, *at the retinal level*, to extract features which are important to the frog.

The four types of unit are as follows:

1.   *Sustained contrast detectors.* Each of these responds to a field of two degrees in diameter in the visual field. These units do not respond when the general illumination in the room is turned off or on. If the sharp edge of an object, either lighter or darker than the background illumination, moves into the field and stops, the unit discharges (responds with a stream of impulses) and goes on discharging as long as the edge is there.

The response of these units was very little affected by the actual illumination levels. It was hardly different when these were so low that the experimenters themselves could hardly see the edge.

2.   *Net convexity detectors.* These were the most intriguing of the types of unit described, and they are usually referred to as "bug detectors". They do not respond at all to a change in general illumination, nor to a straight edge moving through the receptive field. What activates them strongly is the entry into the field of a small object (subtending 3 degrees or less), darker than the background.

Lettvin claims some further remarkable properties for these units. He found that if a dark dot moves along with a patterned background it is ignored by these units, and also there is no response when the background moves and the spot remains steady. However, as soon as the spot detaches itself and moves relative to the background the unit responds.

It should be mentioned that these findings have been disputed by Gaze and Jacobson[3], who claim that Lettvin's bold interpretation of the responses of these units is unwarranted. They suggest that the units can be described more prosaically, in terms of concentric areas in the visual field. It is difficult to reconcile their view with Lettvin's account of the responses to dots against a patterned background.

3. *Moving-edge detectors.* These, with a receptive field about twelve degrees wide, respond to a moving edge, whether the movement represents the encroachment of a dark area on to a lighter, or *vice versa.* The response depends greatly on speed of movement, but very little on the extent of the edge or the brightness of the illumination. These units responded slightly to switching the general illumination off and on.

4. *Net dimming detectors.* These have a large field of fifteen degrees diameter, and their output is transmitted by the fastest fibres in the optic nerve, namely myelinated ones with a conduction velocity of 10 metres per second. They respond to sudden darkening, which could be due to the shadow of a predator.

The two types of edge detector may enable the frog to recognise predators, and potential prey other than "bugs". The "bug detectors" and dimming detectors can be argued to have very direct relevance to the frog's way of life.

MAMMALIAN VISION

Following the success of Lettvin and his colleagues in the Massachusetts Institute of Technology, two workers in nearby Harvard began to make microelectrode studies of the visual systems of mammals. Their early work was on cats, and then, as is often done in neurophysiological studies, they moved on to monkeys. (Cats are more plentiful but monkeys are more like humans.)

The findings of these workers, Hubel and Wiesel[4], were very different from those of Lettvin on frogs. In fact, the Hubel and Wiesel results *do* rather suggest that the optic nerve maps the images much as a television system would, the subsequent analysis being done in the brain. This is despite the fact that the mammalian eye has a greater mismatch than has the frog one between the number of primary receptors and that of optic-nerve fibres.

One reason for the seeming discrepancy is that Hubel and Wiesel were recording from a part of the brain which is not the part corresponding to the optic lobes of the frog. They were recording from the part of the cerebral cortex termed the *visual cortex* (also called the *occipital cortex* because of its location at the back of the head, or *striate cortex* because of its layered structure, or *Areas 17* and *18* of the cortex, the main results being from Area 17).

The cerebral cortex is that part of the brain of higher animals which is thought to be the seat of conscious thought and the "higher" functions. It is virtually non-existent in the frog brain, in which the optic lobes, the largest structures in the brain, are the centres for vision. In mammalian brains, bodies known as the left and right *superior colliculi* correspond to the optic lobes of the frog, and they receive fibres from the optic nerves. In the mammals, however, the superior colliculi play a rather subsidiary role in vision, being concerned with such automatic aspects as controlling the eye muscles to direct the gaze. To do this they have to detect crude features of the visual image, movement in particular, so as to direct the gaze appropriately. The function of the superior colliculi in mammals may therefore be fairly similar to that of the optic lobes in frogs.

The surprising finding that mammalian vision *does* seem to work like a television camera, so far as the mapping on the cortex is concerned, seems less anomalous in view of the fact that visual information is also conveyed elsewhere in the system. The fine resolution of the retina, and the neural circuitry allowing processing within it, would seem to be redundant for the cortical input but presumably play a part in conjunction with the superior colliculus.

The signals which reach the visual cortex are conveyed there through two other bodies (one on each side) called the *geniculate bodies*. All the responses from units in these are concentric or non-orientated ones. That is to say, a response is obtained by showing a spot of light anywhere within a small circular area in the visual field. It frequently happens that a unit responds in one way to the spot of light falling in an inner circle, and in another when it falls outside this but within a larger circle surrounding the first. Light in the inner area may be excitatory to the unit and in the outer one it may be inhibitory. The two areas may have different colour sensitivities.

The visual field is mapped on the visual cortex. In the cortex there can be found *concentric units* like those of the geniculate bodies, but also units of three other kinds. These were termed by Hubel and Wiesel *simple units* (though they are less simple than concentric units), *complex units* and *hypercomplex units.*

Each unit of the last three types is associated with a particular orientation in the visual field, different for different units. For some of the *simple units* there is a line in the visual field such that a light stimulus near the line on one side excites the unit, but a stimulus on the other side inhibits it. Fig. 12.1 shows such a line, with points at which light has an

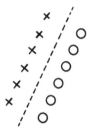

Fig. 12.1.   Receptive field of a *simple unit* of the type which responds strongly to the presence of an edge of appropriate orientation. The crosses represent points at which light is excitatory to the unit, the circles points where it is inhibitory.

excitatory effect marked with crosses and those at which it is inhibitory with circles. A unit of this kind will respond maximally when a light-dark edge is aligned with this line, the edge being such that the inhibitory points are dark and the excitatory ones illuminated. The *simple unit* seems to be a specialised detector for edges having this orientation, in a particular position in the visual field.

Hubel and Wiesel found other *simple units* whose responsiveness could be represented by Figs. 12.2 and 12.3. These could be said to be detecting light slits and dark bars, respectively. It is interesting that the type of unit corresponding to Fig.12.3 is exactly what John Parks built into his character-recognition system to detect line segments as a preliminary stage of processing (see Chapter 7).

The *complex units* behave essentially like the simple units, but respond only to moving edges, slits or bars. They were discovered acciden-

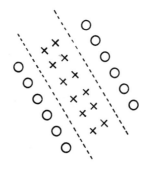

Fig. 12.2.   Receprive field of a *simple unit* which responds to a slit of light.

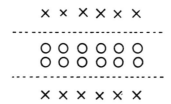

Fig. 12.3.   Receptive field of a *simple unit* which responds to a dark bar.

tally by Hubel and Wiesel, who started to use actual edges made of
something like cardboard as a quick means of eliciting the responses of
simple units — obviously much more convenient than building up the
picture by presenting spots of light sequentially all over an area. They
found that some units responded to the edge only when it moved.

Complex units respond to movement of the edge, slit or bar through
a certain area in the visual field, this area being termed the field of the
unit. These units are not affected by anything outside their fields, so it
makes no difference whether the edge, slit or bar extends beyond the
field or only just crosses it. For *hypercomplex units*, however, there is a
field within which movement of the edge, slit or bar produces a
response, but the response is greatest if the e., s. or b. does not extend
beyond this field. Any extension outside the field weakens the response.

It is rather difficult to see what purpose may be served by hypercomplex units, but it is interesting that one type of simple unit corresponds exactly to something built into an artificial system. The other
types of simple unit could also find ready application in artificial
pattern-recognition schemes.

The response of a simple unit must depend on combining the signals from a number of concentric units. Similarly, a complex unit must combine the outputs of several simple units having the same orientation. Then a hypercomplex unit must combine the outputs of several complex units. There is a progression:

Concentric → simple → complex → hypercomplex

It must not be assumed, though, that all visual information runs along this path. That it does not is evident from the fact that we see the stars in the sky at night. There is not an edge, slit or bar anywhere and yet something comes through to consciousness. In terms of the experimental physiology, it is found that the next stage in processing the information receives inputs from all four types of unit. (To let us see the stars it has to receive input direct from concentric units.) The units of the types reported were found by Hubel and Wiesel in Area 17. The next stage of processing seems to be in Area 18, but as yet no tidy "story" about its operation has emerged.

As Hubel and Wiesel say: "Specialised as the cells of 17 are, compared with rods and cones, they must, nevertheless, still represent a very elementary stage in the handling of complex forms, occupied as they are with a relatively simple region-by-region analysis of retinal contours. How this information is used at later stages in the visual path is far from clear, and represents one of the most tantalizing problems for the future."

NEURAL PLASTICITY

An important component of natural intelligence is learning ability. Most of the forms of brain activity which we try to imitate in artifacts are at least partly the result of learning by experience. Many workers have believed that the way to achieve real Artificial Intelligence was by building artifacts with learning ability. The *perceptron*, for example, has been discussed in Chapter 8, and Samuel's checker-playing program in Chapter 6.

Learning in the nervous system must depend on some physical change in the properties of the neurons (or, possibly, of cells of other types adjacent to the neurons and influencing them). The *perceptron* and other self-modifying networks embody a hypothesis that the changes are in synaptic effectiveness. Any means by which the properties of a neuron might change as a function of its history of activity is referred to as *plasticity*. Much, though certainly not all, of the experimental work having a bearing on it has been done on either the amphibian (frog, etc.) visual system or the mammalian visual system as described in the foregoing.

It is, for instance, interesting to know whether the appearance of the *simple, complex* and *hypercomplex units* of Hubel and Wiesel is dependent on the animal having visual experience. As often happens in biological work there is no simple clearcut answer. Hubel and Wiesel[5] found that visual experience was not necessary for the appearance of these orientated units. Their development is, however, influenced by such experience. Kittens have been reared[6] with experience only of vertical stripes (by keeping them in the dark most of the time, and restraining their heads to an upright position when they were exposed to light inside an enclosure painted with vertical stripes), and another set with experience of only horizontal stripes. It was found that the Hubel-and-Wiesel units in the first set had almost universally vertical orientation, and those of the second set horizontal orientation. The behaviour was as might be expected from the electrophysiological findings. The kittens were playful and would dab at an object, such as a pencil, waved near them. However, those reared seeing only vertical stripes made no response to a horizontal pencil, and the converse was true of the other set.

In recent years a number of workers, notably Wall, have studied another class of phenomena which constitute plasticity. When a neuron is deprived of an input by the cutting of a pathway some way back, it frequently comes to respond to another input to which it was previously insensitive. These effects have been investigated mainly in connection with tactile stimuli.

In a study which drew attention to one example of this effect, Wall and Egger[7] worked on adult rats and recorded from an area in the lower part of the brain on which the body surface is mapped. The area is only a few millimetres across, but with microelectrodes they were able to trace out, on each side, the mappings of the fore and hind limbs of the opposite side of the animal. The mapping had to be traced out a point at a time. The tip of a microelectrode connected to an amplifier was positioned in the mapping area, and then the rat's body surface was brushed with medium pressure until the point was found at which such brushing produced a response from the amplifier.

In a number of animals, Wall and Egger interrupted, on one side, the pathway by which signals came from the hind limb. If the map was examined within a day of the operation, there was found to be a "silent area" where the hind limb would have been represented. If a longer time was allowed to elapse, it was found that the representation of the forelimb had expanded as though drawn on a rubber sheet and stretched across into the area formerly occupied by the representation of the hind limb. The time required was between one and three weeks.

One way in which a "rubber sheet" effect could arise is by physical movement of the neurons in the area of mapping. This would happen if there was shrinkage of the now-unused neurons which had represented the hind limb, and enlargement of the others. Wall and Egger give reasons for believing the effect is not produced in this way; there really is a change in connectivity such that neurons which formerly responded to stimulation of a point on the hind limb come to represent a point on the forelimb.

A change in connectivity can arise in either of two main ways — either by the sprouting of new connections or the unmasking of old ones which were there all the time but ineffective. At the present time (late 1981), Wall favours unmasking as the more likely of these. Neurons have connections made to them in very large numbers, often in the region of 10,000 to a single cell, but the observed responses can be accounted for by considering perhaps two or three inputs. There is an enormous redundancy of interconnection and therefore ample scope for new patterns of connection to arise by unmasking of previously-ineffective synapses.

The *plasticity* studied by Wall and his colleagues is only seen following surgical intervention — what is important is the actual cutting of the nerve supply and not just the cessation of signals in it. It therefore seems a little unlikely that this type of plsticity plays any part in learning. On the other hand, it is not clear how the synapse "knows" that the pathway has been interrupted further back. Wall has recently, and very tentatively, suggested that the effects depend on the fact that, when a nervous pathway is cut through there is also interruption of the fine unmyelinated fibres, termed C-fibres, intermingled with the much larger fibres of the main pathway. There is evidence — at present hardly conclusive — that the C-fibres determine the effective connections formed in the main pathways. If this interpretation is right, it is possible that Wall's results do have an important bearing on learning.

The findings of Wall and his colleagues are of particular interest because they refer to plasticity in adult animals, in contrast to the previously-mentioned work on kittens. In young animals it may be difficult to distinguish effects which are best regarded as *maturation* from those which can be termed *learning*.

Both of these studies of forms of plasticity have been carried out on mammals and are therefore likely to have more bearing on the human nervous system than are studies on frogs and other amphibia. A great deal of work has also been done on amphibia. Manifestations of neural plasticity, including the modification of mappings by the "rubber sheet" type of effect, have been studied in amphibia since well before the reporting of this effect in the adult rat by Wall and Egger. The findings on amphibia are comprehensively treated in a book by Gaze[8].

PLASTICITY IN AMPHIBIAN NERVOUS SYSTEMS

The amphibian nervous system can be studied by experimental methods which are not feasible with mammals. The nervous systems of animals consist of two parts — the *central nervous system* consisting of the brain, spinal cord, optic nerves and retinas, and the *peripheral nervous system* consisting of the outgrowths of the *c.n.s.* which connect with the muscles and sense organs. In mammals, damage to the *central nervous system* is never structurally repaired — there can be a recovery of function due to some form of plasticity, but a severed mammalian optic nerve, for example, will never join up again. The amphibian nervous system is quite different in this respect and can restore connections in the *c.n.s.* after surgical intervention.

Each retina of a frog is mapped on the opposite-side optic lobe. If an optic nerve is severed and the ends left fairly near each other, it joins up in time and the frog recovers its vision in the affected eye. The recovery can be verified by observing that the frog is able to strike with its tongue at a lure waved in different parts of the visual field. It has also been checked by microelectrode recording that the mapping is restored on the optic lobe. The restoration takes place even when the cut ends of the optic nerve have been teased out and disarranged. The idea that fibres find their way back to their old connections on the other side of the cut is not intuitively attractive; it requires the fibres to have some chemical specificity which allows them to join up correctly. An explanation which many workers found more attractive was that the fibres formed random connections and that the restoration of vision was the result of a learning process depending on visual experience.

Some further experiments by Sperry[9] eliminated this hypothesis. If, at the time of severing the optic nerve, the eye is rotated through 180 degrees, it is found that vision is restored but with the 180 degree rotation (and it remains that way). The rotated vision can be checked by waving a lure in different parts of the visual field and seeing that the frog strikes in the wrong directions. It can also be verified by examining the mapping on the optic lobe by the microelectrode technique.

An alternative procedure, instead of rotating an eye, is to interrupt both optic nerves and to let them join up so that the one which went to the right eye now connects with the left, and *vice versa*. Again, vision is restored, but the inner (nasal) side of the right eye maps on to the location on the right optic lobe which previously represented the inner (nasal) side of the left eye, and so on. Vision is then reversed in a left-to-right direction — see Fig. 12.4.

These results seem to leave no alternative to Sperry's view that the fibres can recognise their previous connections (or, for the switch-over of optic nerves, the fibres in the other nerve corresponding to their previous connections) by some sort of chemical specificity. It looks as though the whole thing is genetically determined with no need to postulate any form of plasticity.

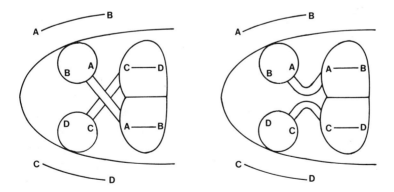

Fig. 12.4.   Showing the effect of uncrossing the optic nerves (by interrupting both and introducing a barrier to prevent them re-forming their previous connections). The circles represent the eyes, and points A, B, C and D in the visual field form images on the respective retinas. After the operation, A and B are mapped on the tectum where C and D were mapped previously. A lure presented at A causes the frog to strike at C, and at B it causes it to strike at D. This represents a reversal of horizontal direction.

That the picture is not so simple has been shown in further experiments, in which it has been found that a part of a retina may come to be mapped over a whole optic lobe, and that part of an optic lobe may contain a mapping of a whole retina, following surgical interference. The "rubber sheet effect" can operate both ways round. (In many of the reports on this work, the term *tectum* is used to refer to the optic lobes.)

Gaze devised a useful technique depending on forming *compound eyes*. These are not to be confused with the multi-faceted compound eyes of insects; what he means is an eye formed from two (left and right) half eyes. He operated on animals to produce either a double-nasal eye or a double-temporal one. A double-nasal one would consist of the nasal (inner) half of a right eye along with the nasal half of a left eye. Similarly, a double-temporal eye would consist of two temporal (outer) halves. It is quite feasible to transplant eyes or half-eyes from one animal to another to achieve these results.

In a series of experiments Gaze formed compound eyes in amphibia at an early stage in their development, before connections had been formed from the eyes to the tectum. When the connections then formed it was found that each half-eye was mapped over the whole of the opposite-side optic lobe, as shown in Fig. 12.5. Each point on the optic lobe (except the fold-over at B) corresponds to two points on the retina. It is clear that the *chemical specificity* principle does not operate quite as suggested by Sperry.

THE TEA-TRADER MODEL

A theory which accounts for all the findings (except the ipsilateral projection — see later) has been advanced by Willshaw and von der Malsburg[10]. According to this, the fibres of the optic nerve do not have specific labelling in the sense of a distinct substance for each fibre. Instead, a relatively small number of distinct substances are produced at separate points on the retina, diffusing out from their points of origin so that the concentration is lower the greater the distance. A given fibre carries with it a mixture of these marker substances corresponding to their respective concentrations at the fibre's point of origin in the retina.

The chemical mixtures carried by the fibres enable them to form a continuous mapping on the optic lobe when they first reach it during

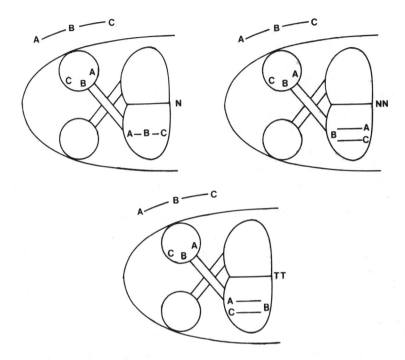

Fig. 12.5. Showing how the visual field is mapped, first on the retina and then on the tectum, in a frog (N) with a normal right eye, one (NN) with a double-nasal compound eye, and one (TT) with a double-temporal compound eye (after Gaze[8]).

the embryonic development of the animal. The way it is formed is explained by these workers in an earlier paper[11] by analogy with tea-traders coming from India and developing a market in England (see below). The nerve fibres carry their chemical mixtures with them to the optic lobe, which then comes to have a distribution of the substances over its surface, similar to that over the area of the retina. If the optic nerve is cut and allowed to regenerate, the mapping is restored because each fibre makes several connections with the lobe, but lets the strength of connection be greatest where the agreement is best between the fibre's own chemical make-up and that of the lobe. Connections to points of poor agreement are abandoned and new ones formed adjacent to other existing connections. This allows the main connection of the fibre to migrate towards the point on the lobe which is chemically similar. The distribution of marker substances on the lobe constitutes a memory allowing orderly reconnection.

It is found that this model, operating subject to an upper limit to the total of synaptic *weights* for any one fibre, accounts for all the "rubber-sheet" effects which have been seen. The tea-trader analogy uses the land area of India to represent the area of the retina, and that of England the optic lobe. It is assumed that tea is produced in a number of plantations in India, each one having its own distinctive flavour. Traders come from villages having their own blends of tea, the blend from a particular village containing proportions of the basic teas which are inversely related to the distance of the village from the respective plantation.

Traders can only carry a certain amount of tea with them. Customers acquire a taste for the blend of tea they have been receiving, and a trader supplies most of his tea to the customers who prefer it. Customer preference is thus self-reinforcing, but each trader is in competition with his fellows and spreads around some samples of his tea to attract new custom. It has been shown by computer simulation that such competition and interaction can produce a continuous mapping, provided the initial contacts of traders with customers had some slight semblance of order.

The necessary semblance of order would exist in the optic-nerve situation because the bundle of fibres remains together as it grows from the retina. The mapping is first formed between a relatively small retina and optic lobe, and is then preserved as both grow with a corresponding increase in the number of fibres. This would correspond to tea-drinking starting in a small area of England, supplied from a small area of India, and then spreading. The spread of the habit in England would encourage the growing of tea for export in other areas of India.

The tea-trader model and its associated computer simulation studies are not normally classed as Artificial Intelligence because they do not have the task-orientated character of most A.I. studies. However, they provide a unified representation of a class of manifestations of neural plasticity and are certainly an important contribution to the understanding of information processing in real brains.

THE IPSILATERAL PROJECTION

The main projection from a retina to an optic lobe is *contralateral*; each retina connects with the optic lobe on the other side of the head. In the frog (unlike the human) there is a complete cross-over — all the fibres from the right eye go to the left lobe and *vice versa*.

Despite the total cross-over, the frog is able to associate the images of the same point formed on the two retinas. This is essential if it is to use stereoscopic depth-perception. The corresponding points on the two lobes are in fact linked up, in both directions. The result is that stimulation of a point on either retina produces a response in the lobe on the same side (the *ipsilateral* lobe), the signal having gone first to the *contralateral* one and then through the pathway linking the two lobes.

In contrast to the primary contralateral projection, the linking pathways come to respond in a way which can only be accounted for by assuming they are influenced by visual experience. When one eye of an animal is rotated, so that the projection on one optic lobe gives an upside-down view of the surroundings, it is found that the fibres linking the two lobes come to connect points which correspond to the same point *in the actual visual field as seen*. The learning capability which is surprisingly absent from the contralateral projection appears in the ipsilateral one. Two quite different kinds of neural plasticity appear to be effective in contiguous parts of the frog's nervous system.

NEUROPHYSIOLOGY AND ARTIFICIAL INTELLIGENCE

The topics of neurophysiology of vision, and neural plasticity, have been pursued at some length. The experimental findings on vision have potential relevance to A.I. systems, and in at least one area immediate relevance — there is striking correspondence between Figs. 7.5 and 7.6, referring to Parks' work on character recognition, and Fig. 12.3.

The relevance of studies of neural plasticity is mainly to the "Cybernetic" or "self-organizing system" approach to A.I.. The "mainstream" work is likely to be related to brain function at a higher, organizational, level. However, the levels should finally link up — as observed in Chapter 1, it was certainly the intention of McCulloch's "experimental epistemology" that they should be reconciled.

It will be clear from what has been said here that ideas on plasticity are currently in a state of flux and progress is certainly being made. It may well be that significant steps towards the reconciliation demanded by McCulloch are about to be taken.

REFERENCES

1. G. Sommerhoff, *Logic of the Living Brain* (Wiley, London, 1974).

2. J.Y. Lettvin, H.R. Maturana, W.S. McCulloch and W.H. Pitts, "What the frog's eye tells the frog's brain" *Proc. I.R.E.* **47**, 1940-1951 (1959).

See also: J.Y. Lettvin, H.R. Maturana, W.H. Pitts and W.S. McCulloch, "Two remarks on the visual system of the frog." In: *Sensory Communication* W.A. Rosenblith (Ed) (MIT Press, Cambridge, Mass., 1961) pp. 757-776.

3. R.M. Gaze and M. Jacobson, "'Convexity-detectors' in the frog visual system" *J. Physiol.* **169**, 1P-3P (1963).

4. D.H. Hubel and T.N. Wiesel, "Receptive fields and functional architecture of monkey striate cortex" *J. Physiol.* **195**, 215-243 (1968).

The above is one among a great many publications by these authors; it gives a good overall picture of their findings. Somewhat more "popular" accounts are given in the following:
T.N. Cornsweet, *Visual Perception* (Academic Press, New York, 1970).
C. Blakemore, *Mechanics of the Mind* (Cambridge University Press, Cambridge, 1977).

5. D.H. Hubel and T.N. Wiesel, "Receptive fields in striate cortex of very young, visually inexperienced kittens" *J. Neurophysiol.* **26**, 994-1002 (1963).

6. C. Blakemore and G.F. Cooper, "Development of the brain depends on visual environment" *Nature* **228**, 477-478 (1970).

7. P.D. Wall and M.D. Egger, "Formation of new connexions in adult rat brains after partial deafferentation" *Nature* **232**, 542-545 (1971).

8. R.M. Gaze, *The Formation of Nerve Connections* (Academic Press, New York, 1970).

9. R.W. Sperry, "The eye and the brain" *Scientific American* **194**, 48-52 (May 1956).

10. D.J. Willshaw and Ch. von der Malsburg, "A marker induction mechanism for the establishment of ordered neural mappings" *Phil. Trans. Roy. Soc.* ser. B, **287**, 203-243 (1979).

11. Ch. von der Malsburg and D.J. Willshaw, "How to label nerve cells so that they can interconnect in an ordered fashion" *Proc. Natl. Acad. Science USA* **74**, 5176-5178 (1977).

Chapter 13

WHAT HAS BEEN ACHIEVED?

Work in Artificial Intelligence has been a spearhead for developments in Computer Science. This is perhaps hardly surprising in view of what was said in Chapter 1 in the attempt to delimit the A.I. field. If this is accepted as the study of ways of making machines do things it is currently difficult to make them do, then A.I. is by definition at the forefront of developments. The subject has an intrinsic fascination which has attracted many able people to work on it, and they have devised new computing techniques as they needed them.

Three topics within Computer Science whose emergence can be attributed fairly directly to A.I. are *list processing*, *recursive techniques* and the use of *formal syntax*.

LIST PROCESSING

In many A.I. tasks it is necessary to manipulate information which is symbolic rather than numerical. For example, it is certainly necessary in programs for automated mathematics to represent and manipulate algebraic expressions. These expressions are sequences, or *lists* of symbols, the word *list* being used in essentially the everyday sense of a shopping list, etc. A *list* in the computing sense is always an *ordered list*. A shopping list is an ordered list if it is written from top to bottom of a piece of paper, but the order is not important in its use and it could alternatively be on separate slips of paper and effectively unordered.

A simple list of symbols can be represented in computer storage by standard methods; it is much like an array of numerical values and can be stored in successive locations in the linearly-ordered storage space of the computer. However, if the list is to be altered in the course of computation, simple linear storage does not provide the necessary flexibility. It is clearly inconvenient to insert new symbols in the middle of a list, or to delete symbols there, and it is necessary to know in advance how long the list may become, so as to allocate a sufficient block of storage.

The list can be stored in a form which is more readily manipulated if its successive symbols are not required to be placed in consecutive locations in the computer memory. One way of achieving flexibility is to let each symbol be stored in a *list element*, consisting of one or a few computer words and in two parts. In one of these parts (traditionally referred to as the CAR for obscure historical reasons) the symbol is represented, while in the other (referred to as the CDR) is the address of the next list element in sequence in the list. A list represented in this "chained" way is free from many restrictions which apply to a list held like a numerical array. An element can be inserted in the middle simply by modifying the CDR of the element before the point of insertion. This CDR entry must be made to refer to the new element to enter the list, and the CDR of this new element should be a copy of the former contents of the CDR of the preceding element.

The term *list-processing* is generally understood to refer to the representation and manipulation of lists in this chained form. So far, it has been introduced by reference only to simple linear chains, but it becomes much more valuable if the CAR part of a list element can be used to indicate the start of a sub-list instead of necessarily representing a symbol. It is then possible to represent tree structures as well as straight lists.

With this extra feature, list processing provides the means of representing nested structures and manipulating them in useful ways. Algebraic expressions are nested structures, in that sub-expressions may be nested within them, and sub-sub-expressions within these, to any depth. If we understand what is meant by:

$$a + b$$

we also understand what is meant when one of the symbols, say a, is replaced by a sub-expression:

$$(c + d) + b$$

and so on. The CAR part of a list element can either represent a symbol such as *a*, or indicate the start of a sub-list representing a sub-expression like $(c + d)$. It is difficult to see how nested structures could be processed otherwise than by using chained lists.

That it is important to be able to process nested structures is emphasised by the fact that natural language has a nested character. A word in a sentence — a noun or an adjective, say — can be replaced by a noun or adjectival phrase or clause. A clause is a sentence-like structure, and within it words may again be replaced by phrases or clauses. In principle the depth of nesting is unlimited, but sentences become rather unmanageable as soon as there are more than two or three levels.

A number of special list-processing languages have been devised by workers in Artificial Intelligence. By far the most famous is the language *LISP*[1], devised by John McCarthy in the nineteen-fifties, the letters simply representing "LISt Processing language". That the language is still in widespread use shows that it satisfies a major need. Not only is the language itself widely used, its influence can be seen in the development of general-purpose programming languages such as *ALGOL 68*, *PASCAL* and *PL-1*.

The most important way in which the new *ALGOL*-type languages, *PASCAL* and *ALGOL 68*, differ from the older *ALGOL 60* is in allowing fairly convenient list-processing. Some further remarks on list-processing are made in Appexdix 1 to this chapter.

RECURSION

In referring to nested structures it would have been appropriate to introduce the term *recursion*. A definition of an algebraic expression must be *recursive* since whatever is understood to be an expression can enter as a sub-expression in another expression. Methods used in processing nested structures must be recursive. That is to say, in dealing with the outer structure (the outer algebraic expression, say) it is necessary to be able to interrupt the process and to apply it in its entirety to a sub-expression. Having dealt with the sub-expression it is necessary to be able to resume the processing of the outer expression where it was left off. Of course, in dealing with the sub-expression it may prove necessary to deal recursively with sub-sub-expressions, and so on.

Some further remarks on recursion are made in Appendix 2 to this chapter. It is now a well-established feature of computer programming in many contexts. The possibility of recursive procedures, and of recursive calling of procedures, has been a feature of the *ALGOL* languages from the beginning. (It often seems superfluous when these languages are used for ordinary numerical work, but is valuable in other applications, particularly when combined with list-processing.) Programs in the *ALGOL* languages are themselves nested structures, and the compilers used to translate them into machine language must operate recursively.

The value of recursion first became clear in connection with Artificial Intelligence. Human problem-solving and everyday behaviour is recursive. When a person undertakes some task, say the writing of an essay, he has to be able to interrupt it and to apply the same problem-solving and planning methods in a sub-task. Examples of sub-tasks could be the brewing of coffee to help sustain the intellectual effort, the obtaining of some necessary information from a library, or procuring of paper, ink, etc. Within the sub-tasks there might be sub-sub-tasks of finding money to pay for the paper, of arranging transport to and from the library and stationer's shop, and so on. On completion of each sub-task its parent task is resumed, the person perhaps saying "Now, where was I?".

The recursive nature of human planning and problem-solving is copied in A.I. programs such as the General Problem Solver of Newell, Shaw and Simon (Chapters 2 and 3). Recursion was an important feature of the special programming languages these workers devised to facilitate their work, and also of the *LISP* language already mentioned.

FORMAL SYNTAX

Means have been devised for representing the syntax, or rules of grammar, of a language in a formal and unambiguous way. In this form, the rules can even be input to a computer program. The program may use them to determine a translation process, or may derive from them an equivalent set of rules satisfying a requirement not met by the original set.

It will be clear from the discussion in Chapter 9 that syntactic considerations alone are insufficient to allow translation or analysis of the meaning of natural-language input. Formal syntax finds its main applications in connection with computing languages, and in theoretical discussions of natural language by linguists. The best-known formalism for syntax rules is the Backus-Naur Form, named after two workers who devised it and pioneered its use. The report which defined the *ALGOL 60* language[2] was expressed largely in B.N.F. and was the first widely-published use of the method.

The general idea of formal syntax arose in connection with studies of natural language by the linguist Noam Chomsky. At the time he was working in the Massachusetts Institute of Technology, where work was in progress on Mechanical Translation and question-answering systems. It is fairly certain that formal syntax can be seen as a spin-off from A.I. studies.

PSYCHOLOGY

One of the motivations for A.I. research is the hope of elucidating human mental processes. The views of psychologists about the relevance of A.I. to their subject range from total scepticism to wild enthusiasm. The work of Newell, Shaw and Simon was explicitly intended to model human problem-solving methods. An enthusiast for the relevance of A.I. to psychology is Apter[3].

The sceptics claim that A.I. work achieves its goals by methods having little correspondence to human methods. The diversity of different approaches in different problem areas supports the idea that the programs work by applying a variety of *ad-hoc* "gimmicks".

It will be shown in the next chapter that there are important features of human mental activity which are *not* imitated by computer programs. On the other hand, people certainly use *heuristics* in problem solving (this is rather a tautologous statement in view of the definition of *heuristics* in Chapter 2) and A.I. studies have thrown light on possible heuristics they could use. The studies have also helped to emphasise important aspects of mental processes such as their recursive nature.

Even where it is doubtful whether there is any correspondence between the machine method and the human one, the analysis of the task as an A.I. project has given a better understanding of its nature. This is likely to be useful in the study of natural intelligence as well as in A.I.

Tasks whose nature has been clarified in this way include speech understanding and scene analysis as discussed under the heading of *knowledge engineering* in Chapter 8. The nature of language understanding has been enormously clarified. Prior to these studies the classroom "parsing" and "analysis" of sentences were presumably thought to be essentially algorithmic procedures. It can now be seen how strongly they depend on non-syntactic considerations. The subject of psycho-linguistics has "taken off" since A.I. studies pointed the way.

The special languages (*LISP*, etc.) and facilities (*PLANNER*, *MYCIN*, etc.) of A.I. allow man-machine interaction of a particularly "natural" kind. Despite their undoubted shortcomings, the methods of information storage and representation in A.I. systems have important correspondences with human methods. Some of these are included what has been discussed above, in connection with recursion and its application to nested structures, but there are certainly other points of correspondence, some of them less tangible. The value of A.I. methods as models of human information processing is not easy to quantify but is certainly significant.

PRACTICAL APPLICATIONS

It has been seen that several areas of A.I. effort are finding practical applications. Various forms of pattern recognition, particularly character recognition and speech recognition, have immediate applications. *Robots* and *Expert Systems* are both devised with practical ends in view, and some of these ends are being achieved.

Interesting further developments are possible by combining the new techniques. The combination of speech recognition with an *Expert System* (and with speech synthesis, which is relatively easy) can allow the "expert" to be consulted by telephone. The idea of an unmanned airline booking office is being considered. As well as making the actual bookings this would be able to give timetable information and to devise routes for complicated journeys. It would also give information on availability of places on flights.

Like other technical developments, A.I. techniques can be put to unpleasant uses as well as desirable ones. At present cruise missiles are much in the news; these depend on pattern-recognition techniques for their navigation. Some remarks about the morality of A.I. studies will be made in Chapter 15.

Appendix 13.1

LIST PROCESSING

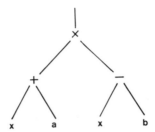

Fig. 13.1.   Tree representing the expression (x + a) × (x − b).

Fig. 13.1 shows how the algebraic expression

$$(x+a) \times (x-b)$$

can be represented as a tree structure. To represent this in computer memory it is necessary to introduce list-processing elements of two types — those which correspond to non-terminal nodes of the tree, and those which correspond to terminal nodes or leaves. An element for a non-terminal node contains an operator ($+$, $-$, $\times$ or $\div$) and *references* or *pointers* to two other elements. Each element corresponding to a leaf contains a representation of a symbol x, a or b. Fig. 13.2 shows the tree with boxes to represent list elements.

List elements are now being postulated which have a greater number of constituent parts than the two (CAR and CDR) referred to earlier. Developments of the list-processing idea allow more complex elements. For example, *ALGOL 68* allows what are termed *structures* which can

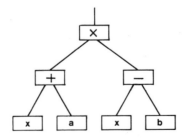

Fig. 13.2.   Tree structure in computer memory.

contain *references* to other *structures* and therefore serve as list elements, and *PASCAL* allows records which may similarly contain *pointers* to other *records*.

A procedure to carry out formal differentiation can operate on a tree such as that of Fig. 13.2 to produce a tree representing the derivative. If the procedure is called to operate on a tree consisting only of a terminal node, it must produce a tree consisting of a single node, that node containing the symbol "1" (one) if the original node contained "*x*", or containing the symbol "0" (zero) otherwise. To differentiate more complicated expressions the procedure must operate in accordance with the rules for differentiating sums, differences, products, etc.:

$$(u + v)' = u' + v'$$
$$(u - v)' = u' - v'$$
$$(u \times v)' = u' \times v + u \times v'$$

where the dash indicates differentiation.

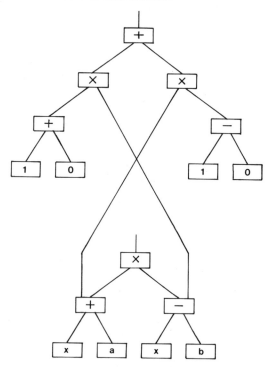

Fig. 13.3.   Tree structure representing the derivative with respect to x. In the lower part of the figure the source tree is reproduced, and parts of it are also parts of the derivative tree. The derivative is represented in a way which, though correct, is cumbersome. Automatic simplification is possible.

Since symbols with dashes appear on the right-hand sides of these rules, the procedure has to be recursive. To generate a tree corresponding to the derivative of, say, a sum, it has to create a structure containing sub-trees representing the derivatives of each of the sub-expressions in the sum.

Fig 13.3 shows a derivative tree which such a procedure might produce from the source tree of Fig. 13.2. The rule for differentiating a product requires sub-expressions from the original to appear again in the derivative. It is not necessary to make duplicates of the sub-trees; in Fig. 13.3 it is arranged that the derivative tree contains references to sub-trees of the source tree, without any need to disconnect them from the source tree. These sub-trees thus serve two purposes.

Appendix 13.2

RECURSION

Appendix 1 illustrates the fact that a procedure to operate on a nested structure, for some purpose such as formal differentiation, must operate recursively if the nesting is of indefinite depth.

A much-quoted example of a recursive procedure is one to compute the factorials of non-negative integers. (The *factorial* of an integer is the result of multiplying it by all the non-zero positive integers smaller than it, except that the factorial of zero is defined to be unity. The factorial is denoted by placing an exclamation mark after the number, so that the factorial of 6 is written 6!, and $6! = 1 \times 2 \times 3 \times 4 \times 5 \times 6$).

In the conventions of *ALGOL 68*, a procedure to evaluate factorials can be written as follows:

```
PROC fact = (INT n) INT:
BEGIN  IF n = 0 THEN 1 ELSE n*fact(n－1) FI  END
```

The first line indicates that the procedure called *fact* requires an integer input which is referred to as n within the procedure body, and an integer result is delivered. The curious non-English word "FI" is used as a closing bracket to match "fi", and the asterisk is equivalent to a multiplication sign.

This example is not likely to convince anyone that recursion is really useful. Factorials can be calculated perfectly well by a non-recursive method, and in fact the non-recursive method is likely to make less demand on computing time and storage space. The recursive way of representing the computation is generally thought to be more "elegant" than the alternative, and more comprehensible to human readers of the program. Methods have been devised for the automatic translation of a large class of recursive procedures into equivalent non-recursive ones. The recursive form is more acceptable to humans but the non-recursive one more efficient on machines. Recursion cannot be eliminated by such means when it is really needed, as in the example of Appendix 1, to treat nested structures of indefinite depth.

The examples so far have introduced recursion in the definition or *declaration* of the procedure itself. Recursion can also arise when the procedure is activated or *called*. A simple example of this can be seen by considering a procedure to deliver the greater of two integers:

> PROC max = (INT *m, n*) INT:
> BEGIN IF *m* > *n* THEN *m* ELSE *n* FI   END

It is permissible to use this simple non-recursive procedure in an assignment as follows:

$$x := \text{max}(\text{max}(\text{max}(a, b), c), \text{max}(d, e))$$

and this introduces a form of recursion since the outer call of *max* cannot be completed until the three inner calls are made and completed.

Barron[4] refers to a notorious function called Ackermann's Function which combines the two kinds of recursion. It is a function of two integers, say A(m, n), and is defined as follows:

> If $m = 0$, A(m, n) = $n + 1$
> otherwise, if $n = 0$, A(m, n) = A($m - 1, 1$)
> otherwise A(m, n) = A($m - 1$, A($m, n - 1$))

Barron remarks that a reader with five minutes to spare might find it interesting to compute A(2, 3) from the definition. The present author has to confess that it took him much longer than five munutes, and even so he made a mistake in his first attempt. The complexity of the task is such that it inspires respect for an implementation of an *ALGOL*-type language to see how it takes the problem "in its stride". It is only necessary to declare a procedure as follows (in *ALGOL 68*):

```
PROC ack = (INT m, n) INT:
BEGIN  IF m = 0 THEN n + 1
ELIF n = 0 THEN ack(m − 1, 1)
ELSE ack(m − 1, ack(m, n − 1)) FI  END
```

The value of A(2, 3) will then be printed out in response to the following:

$$\text{print(ack(2, 3))}$$

and similarly for other values of the arguments (but not too large if demands on computing time and storage space are to be kept reasonable).

Appendix 13.3

FORMAL SYNTAX

The best-known system is the Backus-Naur Form, as used in the *ALGOL 60* report[2]. In order to let the symbols of the B.N.F. be distinct from those of *ALGOL 60* and anything else whose syntax is to be defined, some rather unusual symbols are used in B.N.F. One of these is the combination :: = which means "is defined as" or "can be rewritten as". Another is the vertical line | , used to separate alternatives, and others are the angle brackets < and > . A name enclosed in angle brackets is a *non-terminal symbol*, i.e. a representation of something defined by one of the rules. Characters or strings of characters not so enclosed are *terminal symbols* and represent only themselves.

A *digit* is defined as follows:

$$<\text{digit}> \; :: = \; 0 \mid 1 \mid 2 \mid 3 \mid 4 \mid 5 \mid 6 \mid 7 \mid 8 \mid 9$$

in which $<\text{digit}>$ is a *non-terminal symbol* and each of 0, 1, 2 .... 9 is a *terminal symbol*.

The system becomes much powerful when non-terminal symbols are allowed on the right-hand sides of definations, and particularly when definitions are allowed to be *recursive*, so that the object to be defined can appear on the right-hand side of its own definition.

A string of digits of any length from one upwards is defined as *uns*.

int. (short for "unsigned integer") by either of the following:

$$<\text{uns. int.}> ::= <\text{digit}> | <\text{digit}> <\text{uns. int.}>$$
$$<\text{uns. int.}> ::= <\text{digit}> | <\text{uns. int.}> <\text{digit}>$$

and then an integer which may or may not have a sign can be defined by:

$$<\text{integer}> ::= <\text{uns. int.}> | + <\text{uns. int.}> | - <\text{uns. int.}>$$

in which " + " and " − " are terminal symbols.

Suppose the term "*sae*" (standing for "simple algebraic expression") is used to refer to an expression embodying the four operations +,—, × and ÷, with the usual convention that the last two take priority over the first two. The following set of rules defines an *sae*:

```
<sae>        ::= <term> | <sae> <add op> <term>
<term>       ::= <primary> | <term> <mult op> <primary>
<primary>    ::= <var> | <integer> | (<sae>)
<add op>     ::= + | —
<mult op>    ::= × | ÷
<var>        ::= a|b|c..........x|y|z
```

The round brackets which enclose <sae> in the rule for <primary> are terminal symbols, showing that an *sae* enclosed in brackets counts as a *primary*. The definition is recursive because of this appearance of <sae> on a right-hand side. A definition of a nested structure has to be recursive.

A class of sentences of the English language is defined by the following:

1.   <sentence> ::= <noun part> <verb part> <noun part>
                          <verb part> <noun part>
2.   <noun part> ::= <article> <qualified noun>
3.   <qualified noun> ::= <noun> | <adjective>
                          <qualified noun>
4.   <verb part> ::= <verb> | <verb part> | <adverb part>
5.   <adverb part> ::= <adverb> | <preposition> <noun part>
6.   <article> ::= a | the
7.   <noun> ::= cat | mouse | dog | fox
8.   <adjective> ::= quick | lazy | brown | black
9.   <verb> ::= goes | jumps | runs
10. <adverb> ::= quickly | easily

11. <preposition> :: = over | under | through

The usual purpose of sets of rules like this is to allow analysis of input strings (e.g. *ALGOL 60* programs) which are meant to correspond to what is defined. However, they can also be used in conjunction with a pseudo-random number generator (Chapter 1, Appendix 2) to produce random sentences conforming to them. The analysis process can be said to have been put into reverse. The above rules could, for instance, produce the well-known sentence for testing typewriters "The quick brown fox jumps over the lazy dog."

In order to produce a *sentence*, the generation process must start at Rule 1. This has two alternatives, and the p.r.n.g. has to be invoked to make a choice. Where the generated sentence was "The quick brown fox ....", the first of the two alternatives must have been chosen at this stage.

The generation process must then work through the chosen alternative of Rule 1. That means, if the first was chosen, that it must first transfer control to Rule 2 to produce a "noun part", and, when this is done, to Rule 4 to produce a "verb part". Since Rules 2 and 4, in their turn, transfer control to yet other rules, it is necessary to have a *stack* or *push-down-store* of reminders about unfinished business in the various rules. When the first transfer of control is made, from Rule 1 to Rule 2, the first item would be placed on the stack and would be a pointer to the next item in sequence in the chosen alternative in Rule 1. If the method is programmed in a language allowing recursive procedures, the necessary stack can be an integral part of the language implementation and need not be set up explicitly by the user.

When the generation process encounters a terminal symbol, it adds it to the output string being generated.

Sentences generated in this way from the above set of rules are usually short and uninteresting, like "The brown black cat runs" or "A mouse jumps a quick lazy dog". The vocabulary of the set of rules consists of only the 18 words appearing as terminal symbols — two articles, four nouns, four adjectives, etc.. The method has, however, been used with extensive vocabularies including flowery and emotive words, to generate amusing modern poetry. It has to be "modern" because (a) it is enigmatic and (b) no provision is made for rhyming. This is a form of aesthetic activity, discussed in Chapter 11.

REFERENCES

1. P.H. Winston, *Artificial Intelligence* (Addison-Wesley, Reading, Mass., 1977). An introduction to the *LISP* language forms Chapter 11, pp. 263-286.

2. P. Naur (Ed) "Revised report on the algorithmic language ALGOL 60" *Computer J.* **5**, 349-367 (1963).

3. M.J. Apter, *The Computer Simulation of Behaviour* (Hutchison, London, 1970).

See also: G. Westby and M.J. Apter, *The Computer in Psychology* (Wiley, London, 1973)

4. D.W. Barron, *Recursive Techniques in Programming* (Macdonald, London, 1968).

Chapter 14

WHAT HASN'T BEEN ACHIEVED?

Associated with any area of human endeavour there are attempts to predict future progress. Such predictions often prove to be wildly erronious, usually in the direction of over-optimism. One reason for this is simply the general bouyancy of human nature. Also, there is a tendency to fail to realise how strongly the problems tackled in the early stages of a study have been — perhaps unconsciously — selected to be the easier ones. The problems which were shelved in the earlier stages have to be unshelved if progress is to be made. They were shelved in the first place because no way of tackling them was then apparent; it rather often happens that none becomes apparent even in the light of the experience gained in tackling the easier problems.

It can be argued that the field of Artificial Intelligence has suffered more than most from over-enthusiastic extrapolation from early successes. The great sceptic is the philosopher H.L. Dreyfus[1], who comments on the predictions made by Herbert Simon[2] in 1957 and on other claims by A.I. workers. Some of these can be seen to be over-confident to a degree which borders on dishonesty.

Simon considered that, in the visible future, the range of problems machines would handle "would be coextensive with the range to which the human mind has been applied". He also made specific predictions as follows:

1. That within ten years a digital computer will be the world's chess champion, unless the rules bar it from competition.

2. That within ten years a digital computer will discover and prove an important new mathematical theorem.
3. That within ten years most theories in psychology will take the form of computer programs, or of qualitative statements about the characteristics of computer programs.

It is now clear that Simon was over-enthusiastic, and Dreyfus claims that A.I. people never learn to desist from wild predictions. While there is truth in this, it is also important not to let the pendulum swing too far the other way. As pointed out in Chapter 1, there is a tendency to view "intelligence" in a way which makes any attempt at A.I. automatically self-defeating. As soon as it is demonstrated that a machine can perform some task, the demonstration itself can be held to show that the task is not "intelligent".

There are, however, serious and undeniable areas of mismatch between what has been done by machines and what brains can do.

BRAIN-MACHINE MISMATCH

Perhaps the most widely-acknowledged area of mismatch is in methods used in chess-playing. It is now thought that Simon's first prediction may be fulfilled in a few years' time — certainly, machines are now playing chess of a very high standard. However, the successful chess-playing programs operate in a way which is different from that of the brain. The computer method relies on the enormous computing capacity of the machine when programmed in a fairly straightforward way to explore a large (though certainly not exhaustive) lookahead tree.

In describing their General Problem Solver, Newell, Shaw and Simon mention that they were dissatisfied with its plodding, one-step-at-a-time, way of developing a proof. This is in contrast to the behaviour of human problem-solvers, who are often able to report that they can "see their way through" while still some way from the final steps of the proof. Mathematicians refer to the "warm satisfied feeling" which suffuses them when they become confident they are on the right track. Often this feeling comes when the person is a long way from completing the proof in detail. Sometimes the feeling proves to have arisen prematurely, when a solution was not within grasp, but usually it is warranted.

Newell, Shaw and Simon tried to improve their method by introducing a principle of "planning". The idea was to find a "skeleton" of a proof by the standard G.P.S. method, but disregarding the less difficult forms of difference which could exist between "what we have" and "what we want". Associated with the reduced set of differences would be a reduced set of operators, since some operators would become irrelevant. The "skeleton" proof found in this way would then guide the development of the full proof using the full set of types of difference.

This modification of G.P.S. does not appear to have significantly increased its power, though probably something of the sort is needed in any problem-solving activity. Dreyfus argues that the embodiment of "planning" involves structuring the problem and distinguishing the essential from the inessential in a way which is characteristically human.

What Dreyfus is saying is that "planning" is another heuristic principle which can be embodied in programs, but formulating the principle in the first place in a particular context has, at present, to depend on human insight. The A.I. programs are limited because they do not form their own heuristics. Much the same deficiency has been referred to in discussing Selfridge's *Pandemonium* (Chapter 7) as the difficulty of implementing appropriate *mutated fission*. It has also been referred to explicitly by Samuel with reference to the constituents of the *static evaluation function* of his checker-playing program (Chapter 6); the program adjusts numerical parameters in the *s.e.f.* and alters the selection of terms in it, but does not introduce qualitatively-new terms.

In his discussions of game-playing (Chapter 6), Good makes two rather interesting comments. In an appendix to his discussion of computer chess he makes some observations on a game of draughts (or checkers) played between a person and Samuel's program. Good claims there was a point in the game at which the person could have forced a win, and that the key move could readily be justified by a *verbal* analysis of the situation, but was not "noticed" by the tree-search method embodied in the program.

In his discussion of the game of GO, on the other hand, Good comments that an experienced player is often unable to explain convincingly to a beginner why one move is better than another. The player can discuss the move in terms of "attack" and "defence" and so on, but the final decision is made by some process which has resisted analysis. The method seems to be twice removed from known machine methods — verbal description allows one stage of removal, and the next goes again into a non-verbal area.

The fact that some success has been achieved in A.I. work does not, according to Dreyfus, necessarily mean that the work is heading in a direction which will allow a deeper correspondence to natural intelligence. He talks about a stone-age man climbing a tree and claiming he has made progress towards space travel. Undoubtedly he is nearer the planets (those in sight, at least) than are his fellows on the ground. However, if he really wants to achieve space travel he would do better to come down out of the tree and to set about discovering fire and the wheel and iron-smelting and so on.

In Chapter 13 it was argued that some of the principles used in A.I. (heuristics in particular) are also features of human thought, even though there are many other features which have not been elucidated. If these arguments are accepted they suggest that A.I. workers are not so firmly on the wrong track as the stone-age man in his tree.

PARALLEL OPERATION

Some of the differences between the operations of brains and of computers can be related to the fact that a computer is essentially a serial device, whereas brains operate in a highly-parallel fashion. (Modern computers are less strictly-serial than were earlier ones, since various kinds of data-transfer can be initiated and allowed to continue at the same time as the central processing unit, or units, carry on working. However, except in some very recently-developed machines, the number of processes operating simultaneously can usually be counted on the fingers of two hands if not of one.)

A parallel process can be imitated by a serial one, simply by programming the serial one to "visit" in sequence all the constituent parts of the parallel process. On each "visit" the constituent is suitably updated. The serial system simulates the parallel one more and more closely as the time-intervals between the rounds of "visits" are reduced.

For a parallel system of the complexity of the brain, the attempt to achieve the same result using a serial device may be quite outside the realms of possibility. There is a "neurological explosion", perhaps not quite so drastic as the "combinatorial explosion", but enough to deny the effective equivalence of serial and parallel systems. Selfridge's use of the term *Pandemonium* was intended to emphasise the fact that his system is best thought of as operating in parallel.

Dreyfus refers to the ability of the brain to take an overall view of the structure of a task situation, in a way which allows it to "zero in" on significant aspects while still maintaining "fringe consciousness" of others. The highly-parallel operation allows these effects in a way which has not been imitated in artifacts.

The mathematician Poincaré had some feeling for the parallel nature of his own thinking, about which he related the following[3]:

> "One evening, contrary to my custom, I drank black coffee and could not sleep. Ideas rose in crowds; I felt them collide until pairs interlocked, so to speak, making a stable combination."

Later he says:

> "In this .... way of looking at it, all the combinations would be formed in consequence of the automatism of the subliminal self, but only the interesting ones would break through into the domain of consciousness. And this is still very mysterious. What is the cause that, among the thousand products of our unconscious activity, some are called to pass the threshold, while others remain below?"

What Poincaré felt to be mysterious in 1913 is still very much so today. The highly-parallel action of the brain allows a great many pieces of information to be simultaneously accessible to the thinking process, along with tentative steps towards combinations and developments of them.

INTERPRETATION

People usually look at problems in various different ways, and if possible interpret them in ways they find familiar and tractable. Hofstadter[4] illustrates this by introducing a formal system he calls the *pq-system*. There are three distinct symbols of the system, namely the letters p and q and the hyphen.

An infinite number of *axioms* of the system are represented by the definition:

> $xp\text{-}qx\text{-}$ is an axiom, wherever x is composed of hyphens only (x standing for the same string of hyphens on both occurrences).

Examples of axioms are:

-p-q--   (where x contains one hyphen)
---p-q----   (where x contains three hyphens)

and so on.

The system has one rule by which *theorems* can be formed from *axioms* and other theorems. It is as follows:

Suppose x, y and z all stand for particular strings containing only hyphens. If $xpyqz$ is a theorem, then $xpy\text{-}qz\text{-}$ is a theorem.

The terms *axiom* and *theorem* are used in a formal sense. It can be seen that there is no upper limit to the lengths of strings which are theorems, and every theorem contains one appearance of p and one of q.

A little thought about this system shows that a necessary condition for a string to be a theorem is that the numbers of hyphens in the first two hyphen-groups must add to the number in the last hyphen-group. The system is, in fact, a formal representation of addition. The important point is that people, presented with such a system, always look for interpretations or "meanings" like the interpretation of this one in terms of addition.

There would be no difficulty in writing a computer program to make "interpretations" of a large class of formal systems like the *pq-system*, but this would not approach the flexibility of the brain, which continually looks for interpretations and new viewpoints for anything it has to deal with.

An example of this flexibility can be seen in considering the process of syntactic analysis needed to understand the last verse of the nursery rhyme "This is the house that Jack built". Normally a sentence is very difficult to follow if its depth of nesting of clauses is more than two or three. A computer program (a compiler for programs in an *ALGOL*-type language, say) can analyse input having a greater depth of nesting, provided storage space has been allocated for a sufficient *push-down store* or *stack*. Every time the analysis process goes from one level of nesting to one deeper, information has to be placed on the stack to allow resumption of the processing which was interrupted to go deeper. The information on the stack answers the question the system could be imagined asking as "Now, where was I?".

Just as human beings bring only a small amount of short-term memory to bear on other problems (remembering telephone numbers between seeing them in the directory and dialling, for example), they are not able to store a large stack in processing nested structures. There is, however, no difficulty with the last verse of "This is the house that Jack built", presumably because the regular pattern of the nesting is noticed, and the analysis does not depend on stacking information in the standard way. Computer programs would normally operate in the standard way; inputs similar to the last verse of the rhyme are not sufficiently common to warrant building-in a special recogniser.

The last verse of the rhyme is as follows[5]:

"This is the farmer sowing his corn,
That kept the cock that crowed in the morn,
That waked the priest all shaven and shorn,
That married the man all tattered and torn,
That kissed the maiden all forlorn,
That milked the cow with the crumpled horn,
That tossed the dog,
That worried the cat,
That killed the rat,
That ate the malt
That lay in the house that Jack built".

LOGIC AND CONTINUITY

The discussion of the *basic learning heuristic* and *heuristic connection* (Chapter 2) illustrates another type of flexibility of the brain. It is remarkably ready to combine methods appropriate to a continuous environment with the processing of logical information. (The term *logic* is here to be understood in the usual restricted sense where it treats truth or falsehood of discrete concepts. As the "science of thinking" it ought not to be so restricted.)

The present author has referred to a *Principle of Elementary Exemplification*[6] which refers to this type of flexibility. A number of important principles of control can be expressed in terms of discrete concepts, but have an *elementary exemplification* in terms of continuous variables. For example, the means-ends analysis of Newell, Shaw and Simon (Chapters 2 and 3) requires the repeated asking of the question "What is the difference between what I have and what I want?", and then "What action would reduce the difference?".

A simple servo-mechanism provides an elementary exemplification of means-ends analysis; the difference between what exists and what is wanted is measured as the angular difference between a shaft position and a set point, and the control action (application of torque) is related very simply to this difference.

Minsky's *heuristic connection* is a continuous criterion of similarity between problems. In automatic control, and in what a person does in an everyday control task like riding a bicycle, matters are much simplified by exploiting continuity. A person riding a bicycle does not need to remember specially the action to be taken when the bicycle has tilted to two degrees and separately what to do if it has tilted to four degrees. Instead, it is more economical in storage requirements to let the control action be related to the tilt as a continuous function. Apart from considerations of economy, operation in this way reduces the time needed to learn to ride the bicycle. This is because it is not necessary to do a distinct set of trial-and-error experiments for every discriminable angle of tilt; the learning is "smeared over" the range of angles. A *heuristic connection* is being exploited, but in a much simpler situation than Minsky had in mind.

The readiness with which the brain combines discrete and continuous approaches probably has profound implications concerning the evolution of intelligence. The present author has suggested[7] that continuous processing is the more primitive form of brain activity and that discrete-concept thinking has evolved from it, without displacing it. The readiness to combine the two represents a further example of brain flexibility which is difficult to imitate in machines.

REFERENCES

1. H.L. Dreyfus, *What Computers Can't Do* (Harper and Row, New York, 1972).

See also: H.L. Dreyfus, *Alchemy and Artificial Intelligence* (Report P-3244, Rand Corporation, Santa Monica, California, 1965).

2. H.A. Simon and A. Newell, "Heuristic problem solving: the next advance in operations research" *Operations Research* **6**, 1-10 (1958).

3. H. Poincaré, "Mathematical creation" *The Foundations of Science* H. Poincaré (Ed) (Science Press, New York, 1913).

4. D.R. Hofstadter, *Gödel, Escher, Bach: An Eternal Golden Braid* (Penguin Books, Harmondsworth, 1980) pp. 46-48.

5. I. Opie and P. Opie (Eds) *The Oxford Dictionary of Nursery Rhymes* (Oxford University Press, London, 1955) pp. 229-232.

6. A.M. Andrew, "Cybernetics and artificial intelligence" in: *Modern Trends in Cybernetics and Systems* 3, J. Rose and C. Bilciu (Eds) (Editura Technica, Bucharest and Springer, New York, 1977) pp. 477-485.

7. A.M. Andrew, "Elementary continuity and Minsky's 'heuristic connection' " *Second Int. Meeting on A.I.*, Repino, near Leningrad (1980) — proceedings to be published by Plenum Press.

See also: A.M. Andrew, "The concept of a concept" In: *Applied Systems and Cybernetics* 2 G.E. Lasker (Ed) (Pergamon, New York, 1981) pp. 607-612.

Chapter 15

THE FUTURE

The last two chapters have touched on a number of deep issues concerning the nature of intelligence and the extent to which A.I. studies may be said to capture its essence. There is among A.I. workers a pragmatic school of thought which tends to de-emphasise the philosophical issues. Members of this school argue that A.I. work is making substantial progress, and the best plan is to press on and to simulate brain activity in as many application areas as possible. To do this it may be necessary to invent a succession of *ad hoc* methods. It is argued that, if some powerful general principle of intelligence exists, it is most likely to be revealed by proceeding in this way and gaining experience.

While this down-to-earth viewpoint has something to be said for it, there is also a need to pause from time to time to take stock.

LEARNING

One of the main ways in which "mainstream" A.I. has diverged from other areas of Cybernetics is in placing less emphasis on *learning* as an essential feature of an intelligent artifact. Defining "learning" is almost as difficult as defining "intelligence" — what is usually meant in an A.I. or Cybernetics context is not so much the acquisition of data (a tape recorder is not said to "learn") as the acquisition of skill by experience.

These two facets of learning are not so distinct as they might appear at first sight. Learning a task of pattern recognition has elements of both; the more subtle the generalisations formed in the course of learning, the more truly is it felt to constitute "skill" learning, and the one must merge into the other. The database techniques embodied in *PLANNER* (Chapter 9) and in Expert Systems (Chapter 10) mix up factual data with representations of procedures and strategies. This fudges the distinction between skill learning and rote learning in a way which is probably relevant to the study of human learning also.

Even with these interesting features, the learning of machines does not approach human learning in its flexibility. The evolution of the human brain was presumably under jungle conditions, and yet humans can learn to program computers, play chess, and speculate about the working of their own brains. Most, though not all, machine learning is "learning with a teacher". Much of human learning of skills is done without a teacher, or at least, without a teacher specifying every detail.

The development of a computer program for a not-very-precisely defined task is a learning process, the learning system being the partnership of computer and programmer. The learning capability of the partnership has to be attributed to the programmer, except for a few examples, notably Samuel's checkers program, of programs able to learn on their own. The de-emphasis of machine learning in modern A.I. research is a tacit acknowledgement of the superiority of human learning ability over anything achieved in machines.

Work in the Massachusetts Institute of Technology has included some on a *blocks world* looking rather like the simulated one used by Winograd (Chapter 9), but differing from it in being a real space with solid blocks and a manipulator and observation by television-camera "eyes". The program which interacts with this world is able to learn concepts such as that of an "arch" by being shown examples and counter-examples. An example of an "arch" would be two blocks placed on end with another bridging them. To show that the two uprights must not touch, a counter-example "not an arch" must be presented. This would be similar to the "arch" but with the two uprights in contact.

When the system "knows" what is meant by an "arch" it can be instructed "make an arch". It then obtains suitable blocks from a warehouse area and builds an arch.

This kind of concept-learning does not seem very impressive in this simple illustration. The system starts with a set of primary relations such as SUPPORTS and TOUCHES, and forms its description of an "arch" in terms of them. However, in accordance with the general principle of mixing strategic and factual information, the approach can presumably be extended so that the concepts learned include methods as well as structures, resulting in a very flexible system.

SELF-ORGANIZING SYSTEMS

Many workers have felt that system changes due to learning should be introduced in a more fundamental and general way. Early attempts to make self-organizing networks of neuron-like elements now seem somewhat naive; nevertheless they embody important ideas. Selfridge's *Pandemonium* and Rosenblatt's *perceptron* have been mentioned earlier (Chapter 7 and 8).

Some studies having a bearing on *plasticity* in real neurons were reviewed in Chapter 12. It is reasonable to suppose that the study of living systems might provide helpful hints on how to construct flexible and powerful artificial ones. In fact, as can be seen from Chapter 12, the state of knowledge about plasticity in real neurons is complex and incomplete. Nevertheless, rapid progress is being made and there is an atmosphere of excitement reminiscent of the early nineteen-fifties, when Cybernetics was young and vigorous. The new availability of digital computers and the invention of microelectrode techniques were two reasons for the enthusiasm of the 'fifties. There is again the feeling that new doors are opening and the hope that a valuable synthesis will emerge.

Various deficiencies of current A.I. work were mentioned in the last chapter. One was the failure of artificial systems to bridge the logic-continuity gap as living systems readily do. It has been suggested that the processing of continuous information should be seen as a primitive form of information-processing in living systems — after all, some parts of even the human nervous system are still concerned with it, in regulating heart and respiration rates and so on. If this view is right, the tendency to use discrete concepts has evolved from this more primitive activity. The readiness of the nervous system to switch between the two forms can then be seen as resulting from the persistence of features of the more primitive activity in combination with its successor There is a need to view intelligent systems in a very fundamental way to elucidate these aspects.

It is unfortunate that workers in A.I. have come to be divided as sharply as they are into two camps — those who follow the "mainstream" or heuristic-programming approach, and those who search for more fundamental mechanisms in *self-organizing systems*. The two approaches have more in common than is usually thought; any rule for modifying synaptic strengths or neural connection patterns is essentially a problem-solving heuristic, and much that has been said about heuristics in other contexts is applicable.

There is a need to review ideas on *self-organizing systems* and to relate them to modern developments. Such a review[1] is currently at an early stage of preparation.

MORALITY OF A.I.

Where A.I. work impinges on everyday life, it usually seems to be in ways which are potentially beneficial (or, at least, the A.I. workers manage to make it appear so). However, it should certainly not be assumed that the social and other consequences are automatically desirable.

In the first place, of course, A.I. projects cost money which comes mainly from public funds and could usefully be spent in other ways (or left in the taxpayer's pocket). However, the work need only make a fairly small contribution to the intellectual atmosphere to be as deserving of support as many other activities which draw on public funds.

A more serious consideration is that some A.I. developments could have distinctly unpleasant consequences. Work on game-playing programs has pretty certainly been undertaken and supported with the idea that there could be relevance to war strategy. The recent development of cruise missiles certainly depends on pattern recognition techniques. No doubt other A.I. techniques will play a part in future unmanned war machines which will plan their actions to deceive the enemy (or the enemy's machines) and may wait in ambush or act as decoys. There seems to be no limit to the ingenuity mankind can bring to bear on his own destruction.

Weizenbaum[2] has pointed to another area in which the results of A.I. work could be unfortunate. Most of the applications visualised for speech recognition are desirable ones, but a major qualitative way in which it could influence our situation would be in facilitating wiretapping by police and others. Tapping-in to telephone conversations is technically very easy, but there is one great safeguard for the privacy of telephone users. This is that listening-in is inevitably time-consuming for the investigators. Automatic speech recognition could remove the safeguard since it would allow calls to be monitored by a machine. This could alert a human listener and start making a record as soon as certain sensitive topics were broached.

MAN-MACHINE INTERACTION

As far as practical applications are concerned, it may not be profitable to try to make machines to carry out certain intellectual tasks. After all, brains *are* available, and unless the tasks are repetitive they are probably not unduly onerous. They may even be considered creative and enjoyable by people employed on them, and this feeling is likely to be enhanced if it is known that the tasks resisted computerisation.

Computers have different "aptitudes" from people, being at their best on tasks which are fairly simply specified but involve a great deal of work. In chess-playing, computer methods have won through to a high standard of play by exploiting this "aptitude". Humans play chess differently.

Since machines and brains have these different aptitudes it should be possible to achieve powerful performance in many areas by combining them. This requires careful attention to the interface between the two. It has been suggested that a very powerful chess-player could result from the combination of the human zeroing-in on significant features with the tree-exploration of a machine.

The familiar use of a computer in scientific investigations has this collaborative character, and produces a research worker much more powerful than either the human or the machine acting alone. Artificial Intelligence results show how to extend the machine's share of the work into areas not previously thought possible for automation. However, there is no great economic value in a very high level of "pure" Artificial Intelligence. It is no great disadvantage if a robot occasionally has to request human advice, unless it is operating some light-hours away on a distant planet or is required to maintain radio silence in a war situation.

Expert Systems have an interactive character since they engage in a dialogue with their users. Also, they are not set up by requiring the machine to acquire its expertise by interaction with the real world; the acquisition has been done by a human who then shares his knowledge with the machine. In many if not all areas of application really "pure" Artificial Intelligence has to be seen as something of a "gimmick".

TO THE SUMMIT

Nevertheless the quest for "pure" Artificial Intelligence of a high order will continue. The study has an intrinsic fascination, partly because it is interesting to consider the philosophical question of how far machine performance can be taken. Also, the work will certainly produce useful spin-off in two directions. Like A.I. studies in the past it will pioneer new computational techniques which will then find other applications. It will also throw light on the nature of the tasks, with implications for the understanding of natural intelligence.

The philosophical question was raised in Chapter 1, as: "Are there aspects of human intelligence which cannot *ever* be imitated by machine?".

Work on A.I. can only provide a conclusive answer to this question if a system is produced which simulates a human being in all relevant respects (relevant respects being intellectual ones; it does not matter if the machine does not look like a human or eat the same food). This possibility, if it is a possibility, is far in the future, and for the present the answer to the question must remain a matter of religious belief rather than objective proof.

If, as most scientists think, the brain operates according to the known laws of physics, it must be possible in principle to make artificial systems which simulate it. There seems to be no reason why programs should not be produced which pass Turing's test (the interrogation game) in a much deeper sense than is usually visualised. This would happen if a person felt enough rapport with the machine to be worried about hurting its feelings, or such that the two could share a joke. (James[3] has commented on the nature of jokes and argues that a great deal is revealed about a person's thought processes by what he finds to be funny.)

Of course, if a machine is produced such that a human feels concerned about hurting its feelings, a new set of considerations of morality arises. Such a development could even be seen as a retrograde step as far as practical applications are concerned. One great advantage of intelligent artifacts is that they can be exploited like slaves without compunction; this would cease to apply to one which was really human-like.

These developments are certainly not imminent. Any attempt to estimate how far in the future they may be has to be a wild guess. In an earlier discussion the present author[4] felt obliged to make a guess, which is repeated here:

"It is predicted here, for what it is worth, that Turing's test will be passed in a non-trivial way, i.e. with no restrictions on topics of conversation or manner of reply, by the year 2000. The guess is, however, that even then the computer will seem like a person behaving rather stiffly and refusing to be drawn into small talk. Perhaps by 2050 a computer will seem to be someone with whom a joke can be shared, and with whom the conversant identifies to the extent that it becomes important not to hurt the other's feelings."

REFERENCES

1. A.M. Andrew, *Self-Organizing Systems* (Wiley, Chichester, in preparation).

2. J. Weizenbaum, *Computer Power and Human Reason* (Freeman, San Francisco, 1976).

3. D.B. James, "The function of laughter and jokes" *J. Chiltern Medical Soc.* 7, no. 1, 7-10 (1967). Also circulated privately by the author from The Doctors' House, Marlow, Bucks (England).

4. A.M. Andrew, "Possibilities and probabilities" In: *The Robots are Coming* F.H. George and J.D. Humphries (Ed) (National Computing Centre, Manchester, 1974) Ch. 8, pp. 115-123.

AUTHOR INDEX

Unbracketed numbers refer to the chapters: Numbers in brackets refer to the number of the reference in that chapter.

SUBJECT INDEX

(Numbers refer to pages)